Love is NOT Child's PLAY

TRUTH & TIME, WAIT FOR NONE

Love is not...

Drama: a play for theatre by

sun:jeev

to the love of my life
i hope my love
reached you.

for in love,
you can never be sure.
my life
was due to you,
pure.

Love is not...

Love is not...

forewarn

Rather than hopelessness, there is much optimism to be found in love.

The idea of this story is born out of the first word in it's title - love.

Love can be understood, by knowing what it is NOT.
Really, love can never be taken seriously enough.

You can never take, or give enough of it.
Immeasurable, unbridled, often restless, and exciting. Love is not for the faint-hearted.

The characters of this drama are born into situations of complexity, yet are rescued often by the compelling complicity of love.
Will they comply with family conditions?

Their love, cradled and stoked, at times misplaced, even tortured, searches and seeks fulfilment and closure.

This theatrical drama, with its limited yet obtuse every day characters. Satbir, Samma and Sherrie, comprise the classic triangle - sabotaged by the secret- the truth, that their mothers knew.

So here readers, after all - **LOVE** is NOT Child's PLAY.
It takes two to love.
This play has two lovers, two mothers, two neighbours and two friends.
Time, never an impediment.
It truly, only passes, it ticks- and-tocks.

The story is without a specific location context, for the stage. As is love, without any constraints of time periods, other than the fact that the advent of aeroplanes changed travel and professions in the 21st century.

Like any fearless *act*, *love* too, once set on stage, does not wait.
Well then,
neither do Truth & Time.

The stage is set

Two door frames with a short distance between them, signifying the entry into two houses and the small passage outside it.

From one door frame you enter into an apartment living room.

From the second door frame you exit the stage.

On the living room side, is an entire apartment layout, with a kitchen cabinetry in the background, a sofa set, dining table with chairs and an easy sofa chair in the foreground.

The living room again leads you to a door frame, that exits the stage on the other side.

There are large painted french window-panes on the other side of the kitchen, and the same behind the sofa set, that is flanked with a bed.

S C E N E ~~1~~ child at play

*Satbir Junior is walking back from the
beach. There is sand on his legs. The
spade is inside his pail, which he holds
in his left hand, as he holds his mother's
fingers in his chubby right hand.*

*His feet move in clockwork precision
inside his crocs taking large strides to
head back home, as they climb up the stair
of the stage.*

Mimi:'Stop the dance Sattu, I
should never have told you about
the treat of pancakes with
strawberry jam and maple syrup.'
Satbir:'Ma, will I get three or
four pancakes?'
Mimi:'Aren't your cheeks too chubby
already?'

'Ma, you lookin' such a beauty Ma.'
'Oh so now you butter me up as
always. Just two *Satbiiiir*, just
two.'

'Ma, minus the eggs ma, minus the eggs.'

SatbirJr. becomes glum, and walks quietly, looking down at his spade inside the pail.

Satbir:'Look Ma, I carried two pancakes from the beach, and they have dried up. They are not the real thing.' He points to his sand pail, and pats the wet sand deftly again with his fingers.
Mimi:'Now shower quickly otherwise we will be closer to lunch, then brunch' She puts on her apron to cook for her son. She peels the skin off an apple, and dices the fruit into small triangles into the yellow custard she has set in the morning.

Satbir:'All the tasty things in the world, my mamma has made, are going to go into my tum-tum, after I have bathed.' Satbir tries to knock his two heels together, but lands back on the ground before they knock each other due to his short height.

Love is not...

He is barely under four feet tall at six years of age. His trunks bulge at his buttocks.

Mimi:'You devil, will you hurry and stop procrastinating.' She gives him an equally naughty look in an endearing sort of way.

Satbir:'Ma, I do not know the spelling and meaning of the word you say, but I do love the crust on the custard.' He tries to get as close to his convincing self.
Mimi:'I had told you to practice for your dictation, your English teacher says you can get all twenty right out of twenty.'

Satbir:'I had nineteen last time, isn't that good enough?' he slams the bathroom door as he swivels into a dance form behind it.

He picks up a smaller pail of water, and starts to deposit it through the cracks of the door.
Mimi turns toward the corridor, after placing the custard in the fridge. The pan is on the hot-plate, the aroma spreads around the stage.

She is aghast as she steps into lakes of puddles outside the bathroom, going away from the kitchen toward her bedroom.

Mimi: 'I will beat you up in the evening you little scoundrel.' She beats her fists at the door.

On the other side of the door Satbir who is flat on the ground, stops swimming in his make-believe ocean world. He is like a frozen refrigerated fish, his one eye looking sideways at the latch on the bathroom door that rattles.
The other eye remains transfixed onto the drain pleading it to suck up all the water fast. He has moved the partially filled bucket off it with his hand. He now stands erect, his face glistening with sweat.
There is a back-stage noise of water going down the drain.
Mimi in the meanwhile has brought out his clothes and his school ruler. She knocks on his door again, her own feet wet with the water.

Mimi:'We just bought the carpet for the living room! Open the door, I say open the door or I will break it open.'

She places the plastic ruler, through the gap of the door frame and the door, and attempts to knock out the latch from its

hook. On the other side, he climbs up the
commode.
Noise.
After three attempts she succeeds and
finds Satbir sitting atop the commode
water tank in the bathroom, crouched like
a chicken.
She stares at him. He looks at the
whirlpool of water disappear into the
drain.
Water noise glug-glug sound effect, like
the groaning of a dead frog.

Satbir:'Ma there is a lizard atop
the light bulb, do not enter
inside. I shall come out.'
Mimi: Shrieks, throws the clothes
onto the commode and hastily slips
away toward the kitchen. 'I would
have fallen and broken my back you
prankster. Is there really a lizard
inside?'

She looks at him from the counter top-
through the bathroom door-frame.

Satbir:'Come and check Ma. I too am
scared.'
Mimi: 'Leave the window open, it
will go out by itself, it is
unlucky to kill or hit lizards.'

To appear genuine, Satbir plays with his soft ball, throwing it at the door, acting and mimicking the action of aiming darts at the non-existent lizard. He goes off stage from the door frame.
The noise of the ball, 'Bounce, bounce, bounce.'
After a few seconds, he steps out, his hair cutely perked up in a puff. She glares at him. He looks back at her. Nonchalant. Bemused. Incorrigible. Her heart melts.

Mimi:'Oh hurry up you,..you....never mind, and get dressed and reach the table.'
Satbir:'Yes ma'am. One clean sweet child of yours coming up.' He smiles and winks at her.
Mimi:'Better hurry, and eat. I want you to carry four of them to Balsara's till they are still warm.' She walks off the stage onto the kitchen side.

Satbir goes out of the door frame, and takes a U-turn back and attempts to re-enter the frame.
The two new actors enter the stage and take their positions. It is supposed to signify the next door Balsara's apartment same as Mimi's next door.

S C E N E 2 car ride

Freddy Balsara is on his rocking chair peacefully staring out of the french window, the daily paper on his knees. Mrs. B calls out from the kitchen counter-top.

Mrs. Balsara: 'Aao ni. Come fast. Sattu is here with pancakes for us.'
Freddy: 'I know your prince charming is here. Why don't you eat with him? Pancakes give me gas.'
Mrs.B: 'Oh you *Fatty-Farty Balsara*, you anyways fart through the day. Don't be a grump and come quickly.'
Freddy: Grudgingly gets up, 'You can never read the newspaper in this house.'

He sets aside the neatly folded paper to find his foe on his dining table, himself eating one of the pancakes with whipped cream.

Freddy: 'That's my tin of cream Marukh. Why did you get it out for him?'
Satbir: 'Oh Unc'Freddy, I promise I will not finish it. Come join in.'

Love is not...

The boy is tucking in the second pancake,
while there are
now only two left for the neighbours.
*Mrs. Balsara pours some orange juice, and
one of her heart-shaped ice cubes. She
puts forth the blue plastic glass, which
Satbir drinks out of in the Balsara home
every day.*

Freddy: 'Why don't you keep your
mother's crockery here too? Eh?'
speaks aloud the old man.
Mrs.B: 'Freddy you grump!' shouts
aloud Marukh.

Satbir: 'Oh come now Unc'Freddy, Ma
keeps it all on her glass shelves
out of my reach, and inside
cabinets. Not like you- all out
in the open.'
Mrs. B: 'It's easy to reach son'
her left eyebrow raised. She
gesticulates with a finger on her
lips looking at Freddy, as she
pushes a chair out with her feet.

Satbir: 'So what is the news of the
day Unc'Freddy?'
Freddy: 'Oh don't ask sonny boy.
There's never a rainbow out there,
only dark grey clouds.'

Love is not...

Satbir: 'I thought it was summer.'
The boy looks up innocently toward
his Uncle Freddy.
Freddy: 'I mean in the finances of
the country, you foolish boy. Oil
prices are up again.'
Mrs. B: 'You haven't moved that
motorbike of yours for months now.'

The boy, a bit concerned looks up at Mrs.
Balsara.

Satbir: 'Will you run out of money
Mrs. Balsara? Unc. Freddy here
always says things getting,
getting, '*x-ex-ppennsiv*'
Freddy: 'Do you even know to spell
the word? You must listen to your
MA, and learn all the words and
spellings and what they mean.
Otherwise you will have to keep
riding your bicycle all your life.'

Satbir: 'Oh Unc'Freddy, I will have
a car one day. A red one. I shall
take Mrs. Balsara for a drive to
the beach. She is my best friend
you see.'
Freddy: 'I will be only too happy
my son, I could read my newspaper
peacefully. Will you come in the
morning or evening to fetch her?'

Marukh bemused, looks at her husband. He finally indulges the boy.
The boy rolls his eyes upwards, thinking to himself.

Satbir: 'If I have a dinner jacket, then it will be at 7pm for dinner.'
Mrs. B: 'Why if you have a red car? I'm sure you will have a blue jacket too by then.'
Satbir: 'True that' He eggs them on to eat the pancakes that are left. 'Don't tell Ma, I ate two. They were for you.'

There is silence. The boy looks glum.

Freddy: Smiles, 'Oh *my son*, we won't. You promise you will take me too for dinner with Mrs. Balsara?'

Satbir nods affirmatively as Marukh tears up.
All three of them, have each of their pancakes and cheer up.
The lights dim out, and Freddy's voice over comes in,...'*During those holidays of Satbir, he showed up daily like a rainbow in the summer.*'

S C E N E 3
Raindrops, an apple drops

Clock 'ticks-tocks', to signify the passage of time.

A *taller grown up Satbir*, sporting a thin moustache, carries a large load of books in his canvas bag on his back. He approaches the stage to enter his home alone.
Noise: Rain water

Satbir is in an awful hurry, as he removes the metal chain from his neck, and uses the key hanging in it to open the outer stage door to enter the house. He walks onto stage, removes his raincoat dripping as it is with water and throws it over the tap in the kitchen sink.

He reaches centre stage after placing the needle on the vinyl record, and opens the buttons of his shirt slowly, moving to the pace of *'Chopin's Raindrop'*

He dances along in circles, in an imaginary pantomime as if holding a girl in his hands. Water droplets from his hair, fall onto his face down the nape of his neck and onto his bony chest, falling on either side of his ribs.

There is non-stop noise of raindrops.

Love is not...

A young girl, a pretty one, appears at the window-panes next door. She watches him intently and giggles. She gleefully nods around prancing her own neck, bobbing her head to the lilting piano tune.

She watches him silently in plain sight, but the boy is narcissistically observing himself and his guile in the far-away bedroom mirror. He has no clue, about the bewitched girl.

Satbir
' I have two other uniforms' he speaks aloud to himself as he stops suddenly and wipes his hair with his school shirt.

' I wanna sail my boat, I have no coat, I wanna sail my boat, no muddle, I love the puddle! '

He rips out a few sheets of paper from his notebook and folds the paper artistically, to make his thick paper boat. His head is visible to the girl next door, the music continuing, she arches her head over to see him, but cannot.

He gets up suddenly from his desk chair, slips his hand out of his window and is about to throw his boat out, when his eyes lock with hers.

She simply glares back at him confidently.
They both keep gazing, till his boat falls
out of his hand with the breeze onto the
ledge outside his apartment. As the boat
falls off the ledge (off-stage). He keeps
staring at her.
(Chopin Piano-Raindrops song
continues...till here)

Girl: 'Perhaps a plane would have
been more effective, and practical.
It could have flown away in such
weather.'
Satbir: 'I prefer the rough sea, to
the grey clouds.'
Girl: 'Lightning could hit both.'
Satbir: 'Who are you anyway? And
what are you doing at
Unc'Freddy's?'
Girl: 'Oh I love the smell of
rain...'

The girl flicks her hair away and turns
away.
The boy's mercurial temper rises, and he
feels cross with himself.

Satbir: 'Why did I have to speak to
her? These girls are better off
being left by themselves. Stay away
S'bir!' he guides himself to wear a
long sleeve tee and wonders if she

could see him, neck downwards. He looks at the mirror and flexes his non-existent muscles on his long arms. 'Lanky boy!' he says to himself. 'Tut-tut'

He changes into his long pyjamas and folds them from the bottom, hurriedly picking up an apple, and walks out of his main door to his neighbour's flat. The door slams shut behind him and he remembers the key chain left on the bed.

Satbir: to himself, standing outside Freddy's door - 'Oh Boy, oh boy! My keys.'

Mrs. Balsara opens the door to his doorbell.

Satbir: 'Is Unc.'Freddy there?'
Mrs. B: 'Yes my dear, come in.'
Freddy: 'Oh my newspaper is only half done.' complains Freddy who is in the living room today.
Satbir: 'Good evening Unc.'Freddy, err...what is the news of the day?'
Freddy: Unconvincingly, 'Well my boy, the government is due for a change, so our Prime Minister does not seem to expand the cabinet. That my son is the news.' he ends sarcastically.

Satbir: 'Unc.'Freddy, I meant the sports news.' Satbir is looking around the kitchen curtains to see if Mrs. Balsara or the girl makes an appearance. He looks on expectantly and starts to walk in that direction.

Freddy: 'Oh, My boy, where you going? Isn't *your mother* ever at home?'

Satbir: 'She has the grade ten examination papers to correct. She will be back late, and I was hungry, so...it is alright, I will eat my apple.' He sits again on the armchair, a bit away from Freddy.

He can smell some baking in the air.
The girl at the window, makes her appearance in a changed getup, wearing a longish dress, well below her knees.
She has in her hands a small tray on which are some sponge cakes covered in individual wrapping and round-shaped cookies on a heap of plates.
She places the items before Unc.'Freddy, crossing ahead of where Satbir is seated.
Everyone remains silent, as Unc.'Freddy watches them with his circular glasses on the bridge of his nose.

Satbir's recorded voice-over, in the backdrop, *as his inner conscience takes over* (body tightens up)

'I can smell the mix of bakery and shampoo mixed with her perfume or that thing that my mother applies- What is it...?' he perks his nose... 'Ah lotions!' His facial expressions contort – as he speaks aloud in voice-over *'Who is she and what is she doing in this place?'*

The girl sits alongside Unc.'Freddy who places his arm around her.
Satbir gets uncomfortable over Unc.'Freddy's over familiarity with her.

Satbir:'Have I lost a friend?' speaks the voice-over in a hushed tone.
Satbir crosses his feet inwards.

Freddy: 'Have you met this mischievous girl?'

Before Satbir can answer, Mrs. Balsara makes her appearance from behind the counter-top, with lemon squash in four glasses on a tray. She places the glasses before each one of them and keeps hers in her own hands.
There is silence as Marukh keeps the glasses, and Satbir's eyeballs seem to follow every move.

Mrs. B: 'Come Satbir, help yourself.'

As the eager boy gets up, the apple falls from his lap, rolls all over the ground till it comes to a stop at the girl's feet. Unc.'Freddy with his plate in hand, is about to dig into his sponge cake.

Freddy: Speaks in disgust, 'Let it go'

Background suspense music
As the girl bends to pick up the apple her head collides with Satbir who is in a hurry to gain the apple back for himself. Both the hands tightly grip the apple and pull in opposite directions with force.
As the force is applied, the girl is not willing to let go, when Satbir leaves his grip all of a sudden as if in electric shock.
The girl's hand ricochet's off Unc.'Freddy's belly and knocks his sponge cake off his plate.

Mrs. B: 'Now we have a fallen cake'

It is Unc.'Freddy's turn to pick up his fallen food.

'You cannot drop your cake and eat it too!' laughs out Mrs. Balsara.

Satbir is in a crouched position staring at the girl's feet, not able to look up, with a red face, in a position, as if to propose.

Girl: 'Hi, *I am Sammaya*' says the girl, in her forthright demeanour.

Satbir looks up, a bit embarrassed, his heart beating harder than usual. (Heart-beat background music.)

Satbir: 'Huh? That your name..?' is all he is able to come up with.
Sammaya: 'Yes, it is. Samma for short.'
Satbir: 'Well, I thought that's a boy's name.'
Samma: 'It means time, something you boys can't keep!' comes the crisp reply.

Samma looks away to help Unc.'Freddy, placing things as they were.

Satbir: 'The apple is mine.'
Samma: 'You cannot eat a fallen apple.'
Satbir: 'And why not? Do you climb a tree to eat one?'
Mrs. B: 'Satbir! Let it be.'

Love is not...

Samma nonchalantly hands over the apple to
the incorrigible Satbir, who dusts it away
and still bites into it. Mrs. B declines
disapprovingly.

Satbir: 'I will come when she is
not here.'
Freddy: 'How rude can you be?'
Before he can say something, Satbir
walks out the door.

Upon finding himself outside his flat, he
now realizes he does not have the keys to
his house and it will be some time before
his mother is to return. He thinks for a
few seconds. He goes up the staircase and
sits there silently for a while.

Satbir thinking (Voice-over)
'Why does Unc.'Freddy take her
side? I thought he was _my friend_.'
the voice-over thinks aloud.

He is soon at their door again, ringing the
doorbell.
From inside, Freddy shouts out loud,

'It must be that boy again, Samma
open the door.'

She walks up, faces him with the door ajar only a bit, and without even looking at him starts to speak,

Samma: 'What is it? You have your apple now.'
Satbir: 'I thought I must eat Mrs. Balsara's cake. She is **my** friend.'

Samma: 'Any sensible girl, cannot be your friend.'
Satbir: 'Well, she's a nice lady, unlike you.'

Samma: 'You don't even know me.'
Satbir: 'Oh yes I do, peeking tom, that you are.'

Samma: 'Well, it is referred to as Peeping tom, though I am at liberty to look outside my bedroom. If others wish their privacy, they should keep their window panes locked and curtains drawn.'
Satbir: 'It is stuffy if one were to do that.'

Samma: 'That's the predicament you will have to live with.'
Satbir: *Frustrated*, 'Can you call Mrs. Balsara?'

Samma: 'No', She slams the door.

Satbir attempts to wedge his foot, and the
door knocks his foot backwards.
Before Samma can turn away, Satbir rings
the doorbell again.
This time Mrs. Balsara calls out,

*Mrs. B: speaks as she walks out
'Let me speak to him Samu, you
remain inside.'*
Satbir: 'Mrs. Balsara, my mother
will be away for an hour maybe
more, and I have left my key
inside. Can I have Ma's spare key?'

Mrs. B: 'Yes you can, if you ask so
nicely.'
Satbir: 'Thank you, Mrs.Balsara.'

Mrs. B: 'Satbir, why don't you
visit tomorrow again for tea, and
we will have cakes then.'
Satbir: 'Yes, yes Mrs. Balsara. So
nice of you to call me, this way,
despite my ways.'

Mrs. B:'Oh, it's okay, we are
neighbours after all. And shall I
give you a tip?'
Satbir: 'Oh sure.'

Mrs. B: 'Get some flowers too for that mischievous girl.'
Satbir: 'Yes, Mrs. Balsara.'

Lights temporarily fade out, and the actors leave the stage. Light's come on...
In a few seconds, we see Satbir, all dressed up, applying his mother's lotion to his face. He picks up flowers from the dining table. He walks through the door-frame, and takes a U-turn to re-enter.

Satbir: At the doorbell again (noise of bell ringing)
Samma: Walking out on stage, in a different outfit, at the door 'You back again? Where is your apple?'

The door is only just ajar, not enough for Satbir to slip in.
Satbir hides the flowers in his left hand, out of sight for Samma.

Satbir: 'Oh, today it is Ma who has forgotten to keep it for me outside the refrigerator.'
Samma: 'So what is it then? I thought you come here to only eat your apples.'

Satbir:'I have work with Mrs. Balsara.'
Samma: 'Auntie...,' shouts Samma

and goes back inside, leaving the fragrance of her scent at the door.

Satbir swooning.

Satbir: Asking the audience,'Do these women bathe in shampoo every day? Speaking innocently.
Mrs.B: 'Oh, come in my boy.'

Satbir:'Thank you, Mrs. Balsara' he offers to handover the flowers to her, but her back has turned on him leaving the door open.

She observes that the boy has not come in. She walks up to the door.

Mrs. B: 'Oh, please enter my friend.' she acknowledges the flower he holds. 'Give it to her.'

Mrs. B points in-ward.

Satbir:'I thought you would.'
Mrs. B:'And why would I?'
Satbir:'Well, you asked me to carry them today for her.'
Mrs. B: Places her hand on her forehead-'For Samma, my duffer, Now she has gone in. Leave them here' says the disappointed Mrs. Balsara'

Comes in Freddy, hanging onto his pyjamas
and his loose white vest.

Freddy: 'Oh, don't you try to fix
the innocent boy. Am I not enough?
Place it on the table my friend.
Come, lets look at the newspaper
together.'

Satbir loses the flowers as soon as he can
on the dining table.
He joins Unc.'Freddy, but his eyes are
transfixed on the curtains.
Part joyous, part petrified, Satbir is
fidgety.

Satbir: 'Why is she so curt?'
Freddy: 'That's the way of women my
friend. Harried and hurried' voices
Freddy softly.

Mrs. B: 'You men have no manners.
You deserve worse.'
Satbir: 'Unc.'Freddy since this,
this...girl, Samma is here, you
both are behaving funny.'

Freddy: 'No my dear, these funzies
we have with each other every day,
now Mrs. Balsara has put you into
those *funzies* with her niece.'
Satbir: 'I see, she is Mrs.
Balsara's niece.'

Mrs. B: 'From the maternal side. I could never tolerate my relatives from the paternal side. All of them rude, like my father and his three brothers. Men you see, are like this only.'

Freddy: 'Talk about your own family. On our side, we have the sweetest fellows, *like Satbir.*'
Mrs. B: 'Well, you were not so sweet to him when he was a child. It was I who welcomed him.'
Satbir: 'Aunty Balsara, it is ok, we are neighbours, and my Ma says, neighbours are more helpful than relatives. Perhaps more than your niece too, huh?'

His importance once more re-established, Satbir spends the hour gazing at the curtains.
Clock tick-tocks(noise)
Samma does not make an appearance.

Lights fade out, and Mr. And Mrs. Balsara step off-stage.

Lights come on.
It is the next day, Satbir sporting a sleeveless sweater over his school uniform, finds at the morning hour, yesterday's flowers outside his doorstep. He stands with his hands on his hips, after opening his house door to go to his school.

Satbir: 'Girls! I must say, no style,' he says to himself.
Samma: 'Style, without substance is like sense without sensibilities.'
Satbir: 'Jane Austen novels are for ninnies.' he speaks out without a thought.
Samma: 'Excuse me, how rude.'

Samma is sitting atop the staircase.

Satbir: 'What are you doing here awake at this hour?'
Samma; 'You are not the only one who can lock himself out. I had gone to buy bread and forgot my purse inside. They are asleep.'

Satbir: 'I had actually got these for you' Satbir says pointing dejectedly at the flowers.
Samma: 'Then why did you not hand them to me at the door yesterday.'
Satbir: 'Well, well,...err...' ends speechless.

Samma just looks him up and down.

Samma: 'You have not read Pride & Prejudice?'
Satbir: Very self-consciously,

'Sorry? Can I pass them to you now?' Hands out the flowers.
Samma: 'Do you pick up everything that has fallen and use it?'

Satbir: 'Ah, you have not forgotten the apple.'
Samma: 'If you really do desire to present me with flowers, why don't you get me a new bunch.'

Satbir: 'I have to go to school, make do with this.'
Samma: 'You call college, school here? Can you not miss it for a day?'

Satbir: 'What will we do?'
Samma: 'We can go to buy bread. I believe there are many stores and bakeries here. Let us see which bakery has the best bread.'

Satbir: 'I already know Candy's has the best. We always buy loaves from there, but Unc.'Freddy's I know likes them from Pastakia's!'
Samma: 'Oh yes, that is the name, I have been trying to recall. Can you walk me till there?'

Satbir: 'Er...' rubs his palm at the back of his neck. 'Please do not tell Unc.'Freddy. If Mrs. Balsara tells my mother, I will be in trouble for missing school.'
Samma: 'Where is your mother, my mama's boy?'

Satbir: 'She is An English teacher at the Parish Girls Convent school. Wakes me up, and leaves for work before me.'
Samma: 'Okay, let's keep it a secret. Now, are you ready to walk, or only talk like your tap dance?'

Satbir: 'Well, that was style and substance.'
Samma: 'It sure was, but the boat did not have a chance.'
Satbir: 'Have you heard Raindrops...'

Samma ignores his question.
Satbir bends to pick up one flower, out of the bunch at his feet, and in a swooping gesture, offers it to Samma, gesticulating her to walk down the staircase from his door-frame, before him.
She tips her head down, accepts the flower, and walks ahead of him.

Satbir voice-over:

'Do women have a bath in shampoo every day?'

Samma: 'What...???!' she asks, as if hearing him aloud
Satbir: 'Oh nothing, it's the fragrance of the flowers.'

She slaps him on his right arm, and he holds her hand with his left hand, as the walk away down the stage, hand in hand.

The light fades out.

Scene 4 You give me fever

Samma walks up the steps of the stage, from the residence of Mr. Balsara, lingering for some affection, a brush of the hand, or a peck on the cheek, She perches herself on the landing level above their apartments.

Satbir is oblivious to the expectations of Samma. He remains 'without affection', while Samma is both affected and effected to the point of being distressed. She opens slowly the silver foil from the cookie wrapped chocolates and throws them on the floor, close to Mr. Balsara's house.

Satbir: 'Unc.'Freddy won't like that.' rubbing his hands awkwardly behind his neck.
Samma:'When do we meet next?'

Satbir:'I won't be able to, there's gonna be notes to catch up on for the class I missed.'
Samma: 'Oh don't be a sissy,' she reprimands him and bites her lip, almost immediately

Satbir: 'I can't be your escort any time of the day, every day of the week Madame. An engineer in the making, I must do my time in grade twelve...like a criminal in a prison. Not that I love it, and I don't wish to goof off. Dad left us when I was young. I need to standup quickly, as mum's struggled to bring me up alone.'
Samma: 'Oh don't get so serious, I don't have both my folks. Its my third year here with the Balsaras. We meet only once a year when I am here for holidays. Be a sport.'

Samma, dressed in a short-skirt, lingering, her hands behind her head. She strikes a provocative pose, leaning back on the house door, on the lobby level of Mr. Balsara and Satbir's floor.

She attracts his attention to her cheek, with her little forefinger, gesticulating, pouting her lips.

Satbir: 'You seem to be having a sugar rush...Candy's bakery...I mean... No woman has, has,...' he struggles to complete his sentence.
Samma: 'You are more backward than the girls of today. Can't resist you, can I?'

Satbir: 'Mrs. Balsara can open the door any minute, and give you a good whack.' Satbir is blushing.
Samma: 'I'd prefer your spanking.' She rolls her eyes deliriously, with comic timing.

Satbir: 'Show some haste. My mum would not like that.'
Samma: 'You gonna take your mum's permission or the girl's consent? You are a man in no hurry.'

They both hear footsteps behind Satbir's front door, and Samma quickly runs up the stairs to the next floor.
It is the area between both the door-frames, the landing level of the above floor, going up into the stage ceiling.
Suspense music plays...(Toccata and Fugue by Bach)

Satbir turns toward his door thanking his stars, pulls out his house key, and is about to slip it in, when someone from inside swings open the door.

A girl, with frizzy hair, nearly five feet seven inches tall, wearing sandals, yellow heels, a cream shirt with wavy dark brown stripes and dark brown pants welcomes him inside his own home.
For a moment he looks up to read the house number of his apartment and recognizes his apartment.
His mouth falls open to say something, but there are no words. He just gapes and looks back at her, as she looks at him to give way so that she can step outside.
He can hear his mum's voice shouting out loud from inside.

Mimi (voiceover): 'This boy is so forgetful, and has no respect for time. He's not back from school, God alone knows when he will buy the bottle of milk. Please pick up a bread for me too.'
New Girl: Grimaces at Satbir, 'Your mum's unbelievable, even when unwell. Give her an aspirin, she's having a headache.'

The yellow heeled girl walks out brushes past his left shoulder and runs out down the stage.

Satbir looks up the staircase where Samma
had gone up to hide, just in time, and
finds no one peeping at him.
Suspense music...continues(Bach)

He quickly and quietly enters his house and
shuts the door behind him. He places the
water in the kettle to boil, when his mum
shouts again. She enters the stage behind
him.

Mimi: 'So the Prince is here?!
Welcome to your kingdom. You are an
hour late from college. When will
you take your responsibilities
seriously? Galavanting as usual?'

Mimi wearing a wrap-around that resembles
neither an Indie kaftan, nor a western
robe. Her thick arms dangling out of the
large arm holes, her sagging skin showing
behind her perspiring neck. She has a towel
on her head, her hair wet from the hot
water bottle she has placed on her head.

Satbir: 'Relax maaaa, I'm back.
Just met some friends on the way
back and got delayed as I walked
back with them.'
Mimi:'Why? Why? These no goody
friends of yours. Girls, much
better they are! They take care of
their aunts.' She plonks herself on
the easy chair.

The door bell rings,(Sound) and Satbir
walks back to open the door. Ms. Yellow
Heels steps out from back-stage again.
He opens the door, and first notices her
sandals.
He gapes with his mouth open, and is about
to say something.
She hands out a paper bag to him, which he
fails to catch on time, and it falls
through his outstretched hands.
She gives him a disbelieving look, and runs
down the stage stairs again, as if she is
used to running steeple chases in
stilettos.

Satbir: 'And that is...?' he asks
his mum turning around, as he picks
up the fallen bread and milk carton
off the floor. 'Thank God for Tetra
pack. Else I would have glass all
over my feet.'
Mimi: 'What's wrong with today's
kids? I had specifically asked her
for a milk bottle. The dairy is
just round the corner. Yet she's
such a sweetheart, she at least got
me the milk and bread. Please fix
the dinner today evening Sattu.'

Satbir:'Bread and milk? And she is
your new...caretaker? Nurse,
friend's daughter...?'

Mimi: 'You haven't recognized Sherrie?' His mother finally looks at him with disbelief.
Satbir: 'Cherry? That, that was...the *fatso* I had said goodbye and good riddance to at the station last summer?'

Mimi: 'Well grapes go sour, cherries ripen sonny boy. She's grown up, thinned out, filled out and become so curvy. That's my cousin's daughter Sherrie.'
Satbir: 'Well, I will be...damned.'

Mimi: 'Don't be, she's staying with us tonight, and I have offered her to sleep in your room, I snore too loud, and I can't risk giving her the fever. You will be out on the sofa tonight.'
Satbir: 'How could you Ma, all my things are all over the place. I deserve some privacy at this age.'

Mimi: 'Oh just lock up all your things. Junk in any case. All you have are some vinyl records piled up over that old Technics System. Do clear those undies hanging over the rope outside the window. Pick them up before she is back. They are dry since yesterday'

Mimi goes back into the direction of her bedroom, walking off stage

Mimi's voice from back-stage:
'And ya, we both will have two slices each with eggs, and a warm milk cup. Keep it ready in an hour; she will be back after some shopping. She has an interview with Aviator Airlines tomorrow morning.'

Pop's her head back onto stage:
'So don't be sore, you are already a bore to her after avoiding her like the plague last time. This time be nice. The girl is younger than you by a full four years, and she's already going to earn her living in the big bad world. So lucky her ma is. Here you are still studying to be an engineer.'

Dumbfounded, Satbir stares at the door-frame his mum disappears into.

Satbir shouts out:
'It takes four years Ma. Dad would have been proud, *if he were* here (softly) today. She's not even a

graduate. No one stays long enough to listen.'

He walks slowly toward his music system, and flicks all the records and their covers into the drawer under his bed behind the sofa, signifying his bed-room. He picks up the underwear from the hanging ropes outside his window, He can see Sherrie sashay out of the apartment complex.

He is still stung by her looks.
Voice-over conscience:
'What a transformation! Man..' he speaks out loud.

He unbuttons his shirt, slips a loose t-shirt over his head, and is about to fold things neatly, when there is a knock on the main door.
He places his dried undies into his jeans back-pocket, and hurriedly runs to open the main door.

Samma: 'Can you believe it? Freddy Unc is not back yet, and Mrs. Balsara is a sleeping beauty. I need to take a leak and they are not opening the door.'
Satbir: 'Why don't you go downstairs?'
Samma: 'How unchivalrous can you be?'

Satbir: 'There's a fun-fair in our apartment block tomorrow and they have arranged these portable toilets. Mum is asleep. I can't let you in to her room.'

Samma: 'Grrr...Okay, I will see you at the fun-fair stall tomorrow mister. Don't you forget about me like today. The chocolates were yum'

Samma pushes her long hair back, folds them into a bun, and smiles at him.
He closes the door on her face.
Samma stands outside, and caresses the other side of the door with her two hands.
On the inside,

Satbir voice-over thinks aloud...
'I wonder why I like to be mean to her, even though she listens the most to me.'

He's distracted, as he walks into his room, and plays the light and easy Harry Belafonte song, 'Banana Boat' on his record player.

He moves to the kitchen, places the milk on a slow boil to warm up, and picks up six eggs, out of the fridge. He juggles with two at a time, and cracks one, places the liquid into the frying pan.
There's egg yoke smell everywhere on stage.

'Scrambled it is, Dad.'

He is jiving to sound of 'Daylight come,
and me want to go home...'
There's a ring of the doorbell again.
He rolls his eyes, walks toward the door.
Prepared this time, he combs his hair
backward, then nonchalantly talks himself
out of it.

Satbir voice-over:
'Why do I need to create a new
impression?'
Satbir: 'Hellooo' he says, a tad
bit too warmly, a silly grin on his
face.

Sherrie: Raises her one eye-brow. She finds
his re-introduction odd.

Satbir: 'Your eyebrow reminds me of
how rude you was back then at the
railway station. Just last year.
Classic Cherry. So this is the new
you, with all the old antics?'

Sherrie: 'Don't bug me, its
'Shhhhhherie' You could have said a
better good bye last time; and what
better than a cold welcome today.'

She puts up her arms and asks him to move
inside with her hands, dismissing him
figuratively and yet authoritatively.

Satbir: 'Welcome to my house.' he is left standing at the door frame.
Sherrie: 'Your mum's house, you mean. You just have the keys.'

As he turns, she smiles and then laughs, finding his undies sticking out of his back-pocket really funny. She does not say a thing. He continues to groove to the melody of..'six foot, seven foot, eight foot, punch' as Belafonte croons on.
She places her handbag, which has a scarlet scarf sticking out. She now frowns with her nose going into a flicker.
She points out toward the kitchen to indicate - 'Your eggs are burning.'

Satbir: 'Oh, I will scramble them. Its for your highness. I don't like eating them, but mum tells me- if Dad were here, he'd make me the best eggs. I'm not good at multi-tasking.
Sherrie: 'Not sure you good with your music either. You still stuck in your Dad's era. Won't Bob Marley be a better choice?'

Satbir lends a compassionate ear to Belafonte again.
Music plays on, softly in the background.

Satbir: Acting personal toward Sherrie, as if to take her under his tutelage, 'Music my dear, is memory. Muscle memory, brain memory. I have so many memories of dad, blowing rings of smoke in the air, on a Sunday, while fixing the sink. '

Sherrie: 'You've never seen him. I hope it was not the plumber smoking. What a hopeless romantic!'

Satbir: 'Who me? Women won't say that too often.'

Sherrie: 'Oh how many women do you really know.'

Satbir: 'Many'

Sherrie: 'Oh yeah, sure. I believe you. Like your dad and eggs story.'

Satbir: Amused, 'Well there's a few in our apartment block.' trying to impress Sherrie.

Sherrie: 'Why don't you join me for the interview tomorrow. I will get an escort and you will get to see a lot of the pretty ladies at the interview hall.'

Satbir: 'What will you say? Who am I?'

Sherrie: 'My boy friend off course. No one knows me, I have nothing to lose, you have everything to gain.'

Satbir:'I'm tempted. Truthfully by you.' he murmurs under his breath to himself.

She hears that, and glares, but half smiles to herself. She goes off the stage.

Lights dim out.

A soft tune comes back on, its Elvis, with Fever.

Satbir jives to the same.

SCENE 5 A Lovely way to burn

Its Next morning.

Sherrie walks back on stage, with Fever (Continuity, song in loop) playing in the background. She looks dazzling as red wine in a glass. Her scarlet scarf, matches her bright red lipstick. The dress is tight, highlighting all her curves.

Satbir: 'I'm missing a day of _college_.' He is sitting with all his engineering exam books on the sofa.
'I have exams in a fortnight, and I am gonna fail. No one in our family has ever failed.' Yet his foot taps to the tune of Elvis.

Mimi: (Voice-over) 'Get me the doctor's meds today Sattu. And tone the song down, I know I have fever.'

Satbir: 'Okayyyy! Leaving for college ma...' he shouts out loud.
Sherrie: 'Why these old fashioned songs?'
Satbir: 'Dad's old records, saved up by mum. It's all I have of him. His choice.'
Sherrie: 'What's yours?'
Satbir: 'Music or...'

He looks at Sherrie. She is seated six feet away at the dining table, He gesticulates, her perfume, is reaching his nostrils at the sofa he indicates. He sniffles, with his forefinger below his nose.
There is an energy in the room, a sort of chemical imbalance between them. A grown up adulthood, yet the familiarity of the known childhood of each other.

He says a silent 'wow' and gets both his hands up like a hand made binocular.

Satbir: 'Fab. You got the job girl. I've seen you as a child, disliked you through your teenage years, I dunno what has happened...but, who are you?'

Sherrie: Does not bat an eyelid.
Arms on her hips, she pleads 'Look
all over again. I'm not so
confident. Go and hail a cab, make
yourself useful, I don't want to be
waiting downstairs. Please help.
It's my first job interview, its
not how I look, its how I feel,
What will I say? I'm such a mess.'

Satbir: 'Sherrie', he walks up to
her, 'You look like a doll. I can't
let you go for this job interview.
The whole wide world will look at
you like this when you are working
in air. Planes will crash,
passengers will faint in their
seats. Why don't you study further?
Please don't take this job.'
Sherrie: 'Oh my, what drama, when
did you become mister protective?'
Satbir: 'Last evening,...*purrrr.*'
Sherrie: 'What? Are you hitting on
me?'

He walks up close to her, offers his two
hands. She places her two hands in his.

Satbir: 'The truth my lord, only
the truth, and nothing but the
truth. I say before, I say it
again, You look like a doll.'

Sherrie: 'Now you are really embarrassing me. Your mum will come out any moment, run get me a cab. My mum and I are broke. I need this job, and I get to see the world.'

Satbir: (voice-over)
blanking out – listening to his voice 'I can't let the world set their eyes on you like this. Someone will whisk you away. I swear, if you had not painted your lips, I would have by now...'

Sherrie: Pushes him away... 'You have always been rude. What's gotten into you today? Stop this stupid flirting as even girls do this to pep each other up. So thanks, but no thanks.'
Satbir: 'See, there is the real Sherrie. Always ready to switch back to the old Cherry. Proud one moment, pushes away another. What a tease! Confident on her day, miserable to another.'

Sherrie: 'I was low that day, you were going back when we were at the railway station. You were drinking non-stop the previous evening at the party.'

Satbir: 'Now who am I to you? Why should it bother you that I'm drinking silly. You could have said bye nicely. No affection, no attraction? Only anger. And I am supposed to understand always.
You chose to dance with a random guy at the party, Why may I know? Why call me to get to the party to use me as a date, and then dance with someone else. I knew no one else there it was odd. I got burnt, so I got drunk. What the hell? We fight since childhood, there's been the non-stop teasing. It had blown me away...what with your might and weight' he falls on the sofa laughing.

Sherrie: 'Thanks, thats a reality check. I shed the 20 kilos, didn't I?
Satbir:'You sure did girl. *Wa-whoom.*'

Eyeing her up and down again.

Sherrie: 'Which good boy, would look at a girl like this, with his ma in the other room. And where have you picked up all this vocabulary?'

Satbir: 'From me myself, my lord! I would have to. Looking at YOU like this, not any *other* girl.' he raises his hand. 'I swear! And *BTW*, you have transformed, re-invented yourself, and unleashed my imagination, my speech, my senses...my everything.'

Sherrie: 'You devil. Don't get carried away, you will forget me tomorrow. I wrote three letters to you before I came, and I saw them in your room last night, you haven't opened them.
I was awaiting the Prince's reply since two months. Neatly packed they lie. My specially shopped envelope staTionary. What a waste! Go get a cab.'
Satbir: 'Yes your honour.'

He runs to the door, turns to give her a look, winks at her, 'Swell' and runs down the steps.
Sherrie walks up to the edge of the stage, fans herself with her scarf.

Sherrie: 'I thought he'd never notice. Oh Elvis, when will I get his kisses, when will I be his Mrs?'
Lights fade out.

Scene 6 GET AWAY

Coloured lights dimly come back on
The stage is set up with coloured crepe-
paper decor.
There's a fun-fair magic in the air. Light
music is being tested on the speakers,
Lenny Kravitz 'Fly Away' is booming loud
enough for the audience.
A crowd builds up at the foot of the stage
where Samma is standing before the crowd
and the audience. They are waiting
expectedly for an opening at four pm, as
the poster 'FIESTA' claims.

Samma: 'Its nearly four. The stalls
are all set up, except ours.' She
looks up with disapproval
Satbir: From the stage above, 'All
we need is a pack of cards. Its a
simple seven-Up and seven-Down
game. I will kill it in the moment.
Just be with me in the stall.
Harry's gonna take care of black-
jack.'

Samma: 'I can't just be your arm
candy. You don't give me enough
time.'

Satbir: 'I sat up till late last night to speak to you on the phone, with my cordless receiver, you did not call. If it rings, mum runs to pick it up. '

Samma: 'Freddy Unc. slept with his in his bedroom. What could I do?'

Satbir: 'Here I am, in the now. Lets focus. Get the chart paper drawn up. I will be back in a minute. I and Harry need to change our sweatshirt-s and I need to put on my sneakers. I also need some cash for change.'

He leaves Samma there, and jogs up the steps going up the landing level. Harry his best pal, opens the door to him. They both come into the apartment.

Satbir: 'I'm going crazy pal.' breaks in Satbir.

Harry: Shushes him up. 'Mum's the word.'

They both dive into his room, pick up the records quickly, change into their black sweatshirts, as Satbir puts on his white sneakers.

They run downstairs. shouting out loud, Satbir hollers -'Bye Ma, see you downstairs in an hour.'

Harry: 'What's up man?'

Satbir: 'She looks like a doll man. Grown up under my nose. Such a sweetie, I did not realize it for years all together.'

Harry: 'Who?' continuing 'You mean, Samma? Can you get me an introduction?'

Satbir: 'There's gonna be a rush and Aunt Tiara and Sherrie's waiting man. Walk up to Samma yourself.'

Harry: 'I don't have the guts man.'

Satbir: 'I know, ha ha, overcome it ya?'

Harry: 'You are right, there she is in your stall. Waiting for you since morning, lucky you. You better run.' Harry thinks he is talking about Samma. 'Samma dotes on you man.'

Satbir: 'I know'

Satbir: 'Aunt Tiara's daughter-Sherrie, the girl called Cherry fatso I used to tell you about on my vacays. She dotes on me too man'

Harry: 'I wonder why?' he murmurs to himself.

The crowd of the fair is upon them and there is suddenly a rush of over fifty people placing their bets on the two stalls.

Harry feels blissful like a stud at a farm, with his cowboy hat in tow. With the music playing out loud, hundreds of people sandwiched into the parking lots (Vintage cars back-drop) of their apartment blocks, he has never seen his *Horse-Shoe Apartments* so livened up.

Harry:'Quite a show Sattu.'
Satbir: 'I'm gonna fail my exams...' he shouts over his shoulder.
Harry: 'I will, you will make it again with high fly grades.'

Music: Lanny Kravitz, 'Are you gonna go my way' plays on...
The music stops, and the voice over of DK DJ, brings in the apartment council Chief who blurts out on to the PA system.

'Attention, for crying out loud, the raffle for *Mrs. Pretty* at our Horse-Shoe Apartments entry today, goes to this lovely girl here, Miss, we haven't seen you here before. Whats your name?

Sherrie: '*Sherrie*' she says sweetly, her lipstick lightened since morning, her hair a bit out of place, her tight outfit still making her look ravishing yet tired in her eyes.

Chief: 'Congratulations Sherrie. Enjoy the lunch raffle for two. Do you have a music request for anyone in particular?'

Satbir and Harry are oblivious to all this as the music request is read out by Sherrie.

Sherrie: 'Billie Jean...' as she walks away with the prize walking toward the stall she has had her eyes on. since she tried to enter with the crowd.

She has her appointment letter tucked into her skirt pocket, her red scarlet scarf still in her hand with the prize raffle she has won. She pushes her way forward to the stall to break the news to Satbir.

Satbir: 'Any bets, any bets...no one placing any bets.'

Sherrie places the raffle prize won by her on the chart-paper on the number 7. Neither seven up, nor seven down. She looks *up and down* at Samma, as if checking her out.

Sherie and Samma's eyes meet, and they both for a second look at Satbir.
The crowd around them is jostling for space, but no one else is placing any bets.

Mj's voice comes in...with DJ DK doing a
fade out...this request is from Sherrie to
the one she loves...

She was more like a beauty queen from a movie scene, I said don't mind,
but what do you mean, I am the one.

Harry: Calls out loud, 'Sattu, give
me some change for 100's.'

MJ croons.....as she caused a scene
Then every head turned with eyes that dreamed of being the one

Satbir: Looking at Sherrie,'My
dear, you betting your own prize.'

Sherrie: Comes in over the
music'...if I win, we both can go
out together for lunch, if I lose,
you can keep it and take someone
else of your choice.'

MJ...voice comes in
People always told me be careful of what you do
And don't go around breaking young girls' hearts
And mother always told me be careful of who you love
And be careful of what you do 'cause the lie becomes the truth
Billie Jean is not my lover
She's just a girl who claims that I am the one

The card that open up, is a ten.

Sherrie: Pulls him up from the
collar, 'She's beautiful. She's a
ten, I was just going against the
odds for a seven. You won my raffle

ticket, but lost me. The odds will always be against us' she whispers into his ears (Voice over for the audience) lingers for an extra few seconds, a longish period of *time* for Samma.
The crowd around all of them goes,... 'Ooooo....'

She pushes him affectionately, pats at his chest on his shirt lightly, straightens out his collar, acting as if she knows him since eons of years. The pat down of familiarity and ownership.

Sherrie: 'Enjoy the date, its on me, I got the job.'

Samma looks on at her, smoking hot, looking it, feeling it.
Satbir sandwiched in between, reaches out for the bottle of water at his feet, and knocks the bottle down accidentally.
Sherrie walks away, and disappears in the melee of the crowd.
Satbir goes silent. He pulls out the raffle ticket of the lunch prize at the Fancy Restaurant. '*Lunch for 2*' it stares at him, as his voice-over speaks out loud the same at Samma.

Samma: 'Who is she?' asks authoritatively

Harry: Looks sideways at Satbir, getting what his friend was indicating earlier 'Cherry?'

Satbir just stares on dumbly. Does not want to make a wrong move, as Samma sulks and falls back into her chair.

Satbir: 'All bets are on, Seven up, seven down.' he shouts out aloud.

The lights fade out...

S C E N E 7 LOVE CONTRACT

Satbir: 'Hey Ma, we have made a profit of 700 bucks. Lucky Seven was my number, I won the raffle too.'
Mimi: 'Sherrie's train has got delayed, so you will have to drop her off at the station.'

Sherrie: 'It's ok auntie, I can go on my own, he just needs to help me with the cab and my bag till downstairs. I will manage.'
Satbir: 'What's the fuss puss?' '
For crying out loud, I have won

some sort of money, lets celebrate here.'

Mimi: Raises her hands, 'It's up to the two of you, I think I have Malaria, so I'm tucking myself in. See her through Sattu. Be a gentleman.'
Sherrie:'I gotta head back home, as getting train tickets out of here will be tough. I need to return to join training on Monday.'

Satbir: 'You got the job, congrats doll.' He turns back to see his mum disappear.
Sherrie: 'And that girl there, who is she?'

Satbir: Winks, 'Oh just a one night stand.'
Sherrie: 'She's beautiful, Harry told me last evening that she is crushing on you. Go for it Satbir. She has her eyes set on you, I can tell. This, this what do we have, we are getting into, it will not work. I will be flying in and out for weeks.'

Satbir: 'Is it my drinks?'
Sherrie: 'Don't be stupid.'

Satbir: 'Why will it not work?'
Sherrie:'She's too stunning, look at her long hair.'

Satbir: 'I have said nothing to her, she's a friend who has been coming on strong from the day she met first at Freddy Unc's place. She is anyway not keen to step out for a coffee, as she is too shy to be seen with me. She just loves to dominate.'

Sherrie's eyebrows go up.

Satbir:'I mean I was interested, till I set my eyes on you.'
Sherrie:'So I did not exist till then. Bye.'

Satbir: I opened your letters last night, I promise I will be a good guy and will write back to you. Please share your station address.'
Sherrie: 'Get me a cab. I am all packed up.

Satbir: 'Give me a chance Sherrie.'
He walks up to her and catches her hand.
Sherrie: 'Let go off me *Satbeeeer*. It's the truth. I have no *time* on

my hands. Samma is eating out of yours.'

Satbir: 'But the truth is I have fallen for you.' He wipes her tears.
Sherrie: 'How do I know, you will not fall for another? You have broken my heart.'
Satbir: 'I will fix it back. How was I to know that you will win the raffle? And all this stall and 7Up down thing was set up before you came over. How was I to know you will be here?'
Sherrie: 'My letters *Satbeeeeer*! My letters! I will wait for you downstairs, help me with a cab.'

She walks away in her tight jeans, black slides, forgetting her scarlet red scarf on the dining table.

Satbir: 'A good-bye kiss?', he asks.

Sherrie
She turns back, and gazes at him hard, her eyes well up with tears. This time there is no lipstick to contend with.
He walks toward her slowly, catches her left hand, places his right over her left breast at her heart.

Satbir: 'Ask yourself truly, who does it beat for? I know you love me. I can see it in your eyes.'

Sherrie: 'Where will I find someone better, I can offer you a *love contract* – if you go for your neighbourhood girl. I will wait till then. Let time fly by, I will keep flying till then.'
Satbir: 'Let us see who breaks the contract then, to hurt the other.'

He places her hand on his heart, and brushes his lips over hers ever so slowly, its hardly a kiss, just a caress.
He's into her mouth in moments, and soon is lost.
She lingers for a few seconds, losing her bearings.
She opens her eyes to look at him, his hair over his forehead, his square face brushing against her cleft on her chin.

She breaks away.

Sherrie:'Oh God *Satbeeeer,* what have we done, Why ignite this flame that we cannot extinguish. I'm going to be flying away soon, over twenty days a month. My heart will be heavy. How will I work? I know that girl is spinning a web around you like your friendly neighbourhood Spiderman.'

Satbir: 'I promise you celibacy if you so wish. If you break my heart, I won't be able to be with another woman, I will wait you out. If you find someone better, someone else, someone richer, someone more loving go for it. I give you an open love contract.
You are going to fly over the seas, I am sure many pilots and pursers will pursue you. But promise me, when you are done with your work, we will marry and you will quit your job to be with me, Only me.'

Sherrie: 'Write back to me. Give me time to think. Please let's rush, I will miss my train.'
Satbir: recovers himself, speaks unabashedly - 'I will miss you. And love you for the rest of my life, my Sherrie.'

He pinches her softly on her bottom.

Satbir: 'Take them away with you fast,' Looking deep in her eyes, admiring her. 'You Simply irresistible.'

Sherrie:'It's time you listen to today's songs.' she places her fingers over his chin, feels his jaw. 'You flirt, you are grounded.'

Satbir: 'Yeah, I got that...MJ. Thanks. And you my dear, are clearly gonna be air-borne.'

They both step down...and run down the steps of the stage hand-in-hand.
The lights dim down a bit.
Mimi steps out of her bedroom, with raised eyebrows...rubbing her ears...

Mimi: 'Aha, my son's finally found himself someone!'

She walks up to the windows, parts the curtains and watches her son, below

'Hmmm. Blowing Kisses in the wind' she says to herself.

'You raise them, and then you loose them to these girls. Boys, will be boys. Fickle of mind, strong of spirit I hope. Beware my son, beware, after all-**Love is Not child's play**.'

Lights fade out.

SCENE 8 FEAR MY DEAR

Lights come on

Samma:'Unc. Freddy, where is *Satbir Singh* since this past week?'
Mrs. B: 'Freddy, the toast?'

Samma, quite irritated...gets up, goes into the kitchen area and slams her plate. She walks up to the main door of the house, and walks back. Their door, overlooks the door of Satbir.

Samma: 'He is not to be found anywhere since a few days.'
Freddy: 'Let the boy be, he must be busy on his mother's errands.' he makes an excuse, for his male friend.

Samma: 'I have been waiting, after declining his offer for a coffee. He never asked me again.' She bites her lower lip.
Freddy: 'Why this charade, when you want to see him, agree to see him straightaway, no? Boys don't understand all these games. And this child does not know how to play these games.' Freddy looks at Marukh.

Mrs. Balsara watches Freddy silently but does not disagree with him. She plays it safe, pats Samma on her shoulder, to bear it with patience, and walks to keep all the plates she has cleared. She throws the crumbs away into a dustbin.

Mrs. B: 'Oh there are many more fish in the sea.' It is now Freddy's turn to glare at the Mrs. But he too does it quietly.

They both can see, she is smitten by Satbir, and hurting as she waits expectantly. They watch Samma walk up to the main door, peep through the eye hole, and come back to pace again.
As Freddy hides behind his newspapers, Mrs. Balsara catches hold of Samma's dejected face, and tries to brighten her spirits up.

Mrs. B: 'The truth is my dear, if he likes you, he may not know it. If he loves you, he will come to know it *much later. Much much* later. If he does not, he will not even think about it, leave aside realize it. The nature of <u>truth</u> is such, that it remains hidden, till one of you uncover it or stumble upon it.'

She goes across, toward the seating arrangement, Mrs. Balsara quite satisfied

with herself, sits comfortably on her recliner and places both her hands to caress her dress out.
Samma is left thinking.

Freddy: 'What hogwash was that?' speaking indignantly.
'You either like the boy or you don't. I can see, that you are wasting much *time* my dear to speak yourself. In fact you have spent months just ogling at him.'

He gives a gap waiting to see Samma absorb it all.

Freddy: 'When you want something, you must go out and get it. If you like someone, you must leave no mystery around it, as *time* lost, cannot be recovered. He may have been friends with you, but you could lose to his past, or his future time with someone.
You only have today, the present, the now! Today is <u>your time</u>. *Time* my dear Samma, only moves forward. So must you.'

Samma is left thinking, even more, uncomfortable.

Mrs. B: 'Oh come to me my dear, it is rather unscrupulous of Freddy to ask you to go and ask some silly boy to proposition yourself.
No girl will like to do that. Specially when her mother is no longer by her side, we can always come to her help.'
Freddy: 'Na, na, na, absolutely not. In matters of the heart, it is your own making or undoing. If you like someone, why be so shy and yet so proud? It's our own Satbir after all. Speak to him.'

Mrs. B: 'Oh don't you crush her heart like this. What if he says no?'

Her retort is almost immediate and forbidding with a scowl.

Freddy: 'That's always the proverbial fear. If you fear, then don't love my dear.' A serene Freddy looks at Samma with his questioning eyes.

Samma is left thinking.
The lights dim out.

SCENE 9 THE MONEY

It is dark on stage
There's a knock at the door.
Then again. 'Knock-knock.'

The lights come on.
It is Samma who gets out of her bed, her
night dress short till her knees. Her hair
is ruffled.

Freddy: Calls out from inside,
'Who's looking?'
Samma: 'I will take it Unc.
Freddy.'

Mrs. B: 'Groans', and there is a
sound, like a slow passing of a
fart, as if a small gush of air
passing through a crack in the
door.

Samma rolls her eyes, then rubs them, and
in the same action opens the door, as she
finds Satbir outside, about to knock again.
Samma pulls her cardigan over her chest.
Satbir does not seem to even notice, as he
is habituated to walk into the Balsara
house.

Satbir: 'Oh Samma, you have to help
me. I need a hundred bucks, I must
catch the bus today. I must leave

in an hour before mother wakes up.
She will be gone from the hotel for
her flight, she has a proposal, and
she must consider it.'

Samma sits on the chair that Unc. Freddy
usually occupies, lost in it like a scared
squirrel on a throne. Her cardigan slips
from her hands, buttons all open.
Satbir does not seem to notice her cleavage
showing, nor does he bother about the
sadness on her face.

Samma: 'Who, what, where...' her
voice trails off.

Satbir:'I need to see her today.
She has a proposal. I could not
sleep the entire night, I have to
see her, I have, I have to ask her,
I, I...can't you see here. I need a
hundred bucks. I cannot stand here
the entire morning begging of you.
You either have it, or you don't?'

Samma: 'What did you do with all
the money you made from the
fair...'
Satbir: 'Did Unc.'Freddy not tell
you, I got her a ring. I cannot
show it to you, it *will be a bad
omen*. Please help me here, I'm
running out of *time* Samma. I hardly

have any left. Neither money, nor time.'

Samma: 'Who is this person. What ring?'

Samma holds back her tears, visibly upset. Her hands wrung around the ends of her cardigan.

Satbir: 'Oh it's heady this love, this feeling. I cannot stop thinking about her. I never ever,...I mean, ever never thought, that such a time would come in my life; that she would intoxicate me, exasperate me, and leave me so, so...out of tune with my self.

Samma is left gaping at him.

Satbir: 'Love is like a melody, so addictive, so much joy, it rings through my heart, it wakes my spirit, without letting my mind rest. The tune of love so stuck in my mind you know- it is like listening to the same song – again and again and again.'

Samma gapes at him...still wringing her hands onto the edges of her cardigan, not self conscious anymore of her dress above her knees.

Satbir:'You have it, or you do not?'

Samma: 'Oh I do have it, my Satbir. I do. *I have it for you*. Not just the money though, but I know all you need is a hundred bucks you said? Am I right.?'

Satbir: 'Well yeah, I mean, thats all I need now...'he now looks at her top to toe...and trails his gaze off, looking out of the window.

He then slowly turns back towards the house door...which is still left ajar. Out of decency, he goes and stands at the edge of the door, and turns again out of immediacy.

Satbir: 'I did not mean to wake you up, but you know, I haven't slept the entire night, thinking, if she,...if she, accepts the proposal she has got, then what use will be my ring to me.'

He looks down at her feet, crestfallen, as if his own ring is not good enough, as bad as, his non-existent proposal for Samma.'

Samma: 'You have not asked 'her' yet?'expectant, suddenly hopeful.

Satbir: 'Oh no, I could not ask her itself of the hundred bucks you know. I could only ask you or my pal Unc.'Freddy...but I'm worried he would tell Mrs. Balsara and then she would tell Ma...'

Samma: 'Stupid Satbir, I mean the proposal.'

Satbir: 'Oh that. Shoot. I mean, what?' totally confused and stressed out, Satbir lets out a gush of air from his mouth.

Samma: 'Wait here.'

Samma disappears inside. Satbir paces about to and fro from the door, and catches the end of it, rubbing his palms sweat on the edges of the door.

She is back in an instant.

Samma: 'Here it is, two hundred bucks, so that you can come back too.'

Satbir:'Oh thank you so much Samma...I will, I will, see you soon...' he gushes as he pulls the two cash bills out of her hands,

He is about to hug her. She stalls him. He backs-up and runs out of the door, leaving it wide open.

Samma collapses on the sofa chair.

Lights dim out.

SCENE ~~10~~ The Proposal

The lights come on.

Sherrie, is in uniform. She has a stroller
bag at her feet, the handle pulled upwards.
Her uniform scarf tied around her neck.
Satbir walks in speedily from her back, and
suddenly stops dead in his tracks.

She has not seen him, but he looks at her
get restless waiting.
He watches her intently from her back.

Satbir, feeling more sure of himself,
pockets the ring.

Sherrie: 'My transport will be here
any minute, and this idiot is not
here yet. What can be so important
that he has to wake me an entire
hour before?'

Satbir continues to listen. Intrigued, he
raises his eye-brows.
She walks away a few steps from her bag,
toward the audience.

Sherrie: Looking at the stage
audience 'I had told him, there is
no point in this, there is no

future. I do not have the *time* for all this. It is all so confusing. There are proposals coming to me from left right and centre.

Mum wants me to marry a wealthy man. She even asked a Merchant Navy Captain, a perpetual drunk, to come over to my office to propose.

He's been following up with her since. I had told this idiot, to do something, but he kept dilly-dallying that time.

Then there is this pilot in my firm, who keeps asking for my hand in marriage.

A year of flying hasn't passed. What is the hurry with these guys?

You go out for a dance with them, and sit for dinner, and they think you are easy pickings. If the passengers on the plane were not enough...now, now we have this, this idiot.'

Satbir takes a few steps back.

Sherrie: Continues, 'When I used to write letters to him, he would take months to read and reply. There was one, in which I sent him the choicest of my expletives...the duck-muck types.
Thankfully he never read that one, yet he completely ignored me.'

There is silence. Satbir smiles to himself, remembering that letter, and shrugs his shoulders with a 'what is a guy supposed to do' kind of expression.

Sherrie: (*continues to address the audience*) 'On my next trip, I met him at one of our common family friends marriage. While on the previous trip, he was a complete teetotaller, the proverbial good student, the high flyer, this time, he was drinking.

That too like a fish. The crazy boy, would not speak to me, and keep repeating the same *drinks, on and on – over five large drinks he could down in an hour*. It was so irritating. I thought I would never see his face again.'

Satbir winks at the audience.

Sherrie: 'Then there is the fun-fair, and I see him with this, this other girl. Long hair, skin tone like a peach, while I'm raging with anger and pimples on my forehead. I with my blunt haircut, restraining my honest opinion to him. What does this boy do? He takes me by surprise and, and, in his own home... kisses me.'

Satbir walks up to her bag, and holds it from the handle, softly pressing it down. She places her face in her hands.

Satbir: 'Sherrie. You will be late. We do not have time.'
Sherrie: She turns. 'Oh my gosh. When did you come?'

Satbir: 'Just when you were calling me an idiot'
Sherrie: 'I never want to see you again. Let's not complicate these things.'

Satbir: 'What?'
Sherrie: 'Mum will be here any minute, with that Major from the Army, she brings forth one proposal every trip I am here.'

Satbir: 'She should open a professional marriage bureau. So early in the morning?'
Sherrie: 'You are here so early in the morning!'

Satbir: 'So what I do, your mum must outdo. You plan to accept the proposal?'

Sherrie: 'He has booked himself on my flight, and mom wants me to travel with him in a car to the airport. There will be the usual awkward question and answers, it is so cumbersome. Mum never understands at least you should.'

Satbir: 'Your mum is coming by sea, by air and by foot. Chief of Staff for marriages!'
Sherrie: '*Satbeeeeeer*!'

Satbir: 'Easy-easy. Just say no-not interested, I am hooked, line and sinker'
Sherrie: 'The crew transport has left the hotel already. I will not be back for three weeks.'

Satbir: On a serious note, 'So when do we meet again Sherrie?'

Sherrie: 'Never after this.'
Satbir: 'Why?'

Sherrie: 'Mum slapped me last night. You just don't take all this seriously.'
Satbir: 'You serious? What? How dare she? You are an adult major.'

Sherrie: 'Your mother called her up.'
Satbir: '*Whattttt* again?' bewildered, Satbir's mouth opens up. Aghast.

Sherrie: 'Satbir, I cannot do this. I have to work every week, and every few days I'm in a different city. I can't sleep, I can't work, I can't eat.'
Satbir: 'Calm down Sherrie.'

Sherrie: 'I can't. You were my confidante. Since our young age, I would write to you, come to you for all my troubles. For advise. For, for....'
Satbir: 'Love? Just a little bit of understanding? Loving?'

Sherie is silent.

Love is not...

Sherrie: 'Our mothers don't understand. Oh where our our dads?'

Satbir staring...looks at her silently.

Sherrie: 'Whaaaaattt?' goes off like a whistle.
Satbir: 'Sherie, we know each other from forever. What are the odds, we would meet the way we did? What happened happened. You remember I held your hand at Ruskin's marriage, and you pulled away...'

Sherrie: 'Yes, you had your blue tie on. It was gifted by me.'
Satbir: 'Exactly. I vividly remember, but then your letter blew me away.'

Sherrie:'I know. My bad.'
Satbir:'Sherrie, I have not slept the entire night.'
Sherrie: *'Whatt??'*

Satbir: 'The kiss, I could not forget, I could not get it, I could not get **you** out of my mind, the entire night.'
Sherrie:'Oh you foolish boy...'

Satbir: 'Really?'

Sherrie: '*Satbeeeeeer*, this won't work. It was, it was a one off.'

Satbir: 'Tell me you do not wish to hug me good bye.'
Sherrie:'I don't'

Satbir:'Really?'
Sherrie: 'Really.'

Satbir:'Ok, in that case, here is my good-bye gift to you. If we meet after three weeks, we start to carry on. If we do not meet, then you carry on with whomsoever Tom, Dick and Harry, who keeps hitting on you. Or the uncles that your Mum gets before you with proposals. Just remember that if you do end up marrying one of them, I won't see you any more.'

Sherrie: 'It's not like this *Satbeeeeeer*. Don't make this more difficult than it already is for me.'

Satbir: 'Why? You will need my advise after marriage too?'
Sherrie: 'You cannot stop talking with me. Or seeing me. Who will I confide in?'

Satbir: 'Earlier you just said we need to stop meeting, make up your mind.'

Sherrie falls silent.

Satbir: 'Your mother could slap you, to marry you off to the next wealthy guy who shows up on your door. Do you wish to be with a drunk? The choice is yours. I would say hold on, give it time, and if after a year you are still there, I will keep waiting for you. Till then, lets meet for coffee every time you fly in.'

Sherrie: 'A girl's got to eat too you know? The hotel and flight food gets, bland and boring.
You in the meanwhile will not get entangled with anyone else?
Including your favourite neighbourhood spider-woman?'

Satbir: 'I cant get you home food, but I will join you for lunch when you are back. **YOU** don't trust *ME*?? That's nice. You know I have never been the girl crazy, skirt chasing kind.'

Sherrie: 'It's difficult.'
Satbir: 'Say yes.' Satbir pops the
ring.

Sherrie: Hands on her mouth,
'*Whattttt?*' goes Sherrie. She
starts getting mushy looking at the
ring as if it is a wild flower.

Satbir: 'Its just a ring, but its
from me, and it will help you keep
some proposals off. It will take us
time, to marry, but the time shall
come.'
Sherrie: 'Satbir, I don't know what
to say'

Satbir: 'Don't. Think.'
Sherrie: 'I mean, I, I am going on
a flight...'

Satbir: 'Does the dress code not
permit it? I know you met to break
off...either way it will be
finished if you do not accept. Lets
meet after three weeks...think it
out till then.'

Satbir trails off...as he can hear a hustle
of footsteps.

Sherie looks at him recede behind the
window panes, climbing out of the large
french windows.
*Her burly mother comes onto the stage,
with a short man, with a crooked nose in
an Army uniform. She eggs him on to pick
up Sherrie's bag which he does, trying to
shake her hand. Sherrie does not offer her
hand. Her mother looks at her in anger.*
They walk a few steps.

Sherrie looks back, toward Satbir,
helpless, remorseful and yet happy within.
She looks at him and nods with glee.

He smiles back at her, and moves his
fingers 1-2-3, signalling the passage of
time ahead.
She nods back at him, as she trails behind
her mother and the Army man.

Sherrie: 'Yes...' she says. Showing
off her finger with his ring on,

Sherrie walks off the stage.
Satbir comes out of hiding...and lands on
his two knees,

Satbir: '*Yipppeee Dippie Dipsy do,
bubala-blooooooooo!!!!*' he shouts.

The lights on stage fade out momentarily.
Satbir's childhood friend, Harry walks in
and takes position.

Harry: 'Where have you been Satbir, its _been months_.'
Satbir: 'Oh Harry, I'm on the top of the world!'
Harry: 'Sattu, I wanted to speak to you, man.'

Satbir: 'You are my man, but before you shoot, let me tell you. Sherrie has accepted my proposal man a month ago! We are an item! I just got her postcard from Amsterdam, before she flew out again.'

Suspense music. He looks at his friend, expecting an overjoyed reaction. Harry just looks back pale.

Satbir: 'Whats the matter man? You not happy for your friend?'
Harry: 'It's not that Satbir. You have moved so fast. I thought, it was someone else.'

Satbir: 'Who?'
Harry: 'You know who!'
Satbir: 'No I don't! Who?'

Harry; Sheepishly, 'You seem to have forgotten all your time with Samma. She keeps waiting on you, and asking for you. It seems you

don't visit Unc.'Freddy as much, so
I thought let me come and ask you
over.'
Satbir: 'Oh her, I mean we had a
connection; but she would not step
out for a harmless cup of coffee
man. Which generation is she living
in? I asked her a few times. It was
just sheer timing, that Sherrie
landed in my life at exactly that
time.'
Harry: 'But did you not claim you
love her. You were so excited
during the fair. She gave
Unc.'Freddy another impression,
that it was you who
suddenly...kinda changed your
mind.'

Satbir: 'No I did not. I cannot
deny there was an infatuation.
To move forward from that, she
needed to at least acknowledge my
liking her as a friend. She's my
neighbours relative man, she needs
to step out of the house for me to
meet more often, talk to her. I
feel I still don't get to know her
entirely.'

Harry: 'So you just looking for
physical, proximity eh? Sherrie

bagged you? Or the other way round?'

Satbir; 'No thats not what I mean; I mean, why does it have to straightaway imply that. Yes, eventually, that too, there needs to be some chemistry before any physics or biology. I can just say we are very good childhood friends. Extremely fond of each other. While with Samma, we *were* good friends. Now a man can't be very good friends at this stage with two girls at the same time. It's just not fair, not true. I could not risk losing Sherrie to someone else. It would have devastated me and her too.'

Harry: 'Well, you are in one helluva speed man. Switching tracks.'
Satbir: 'The bond with Sherrie is very different, she understands me, and unravels me, in a fashion, that I myself have not known. She challenges me in a sort of equal way. On music, on Mum-Dad issues. She has her own thought process, and expects me to have my own.'

Harry: 'Was Samma a push-over then?'
Satbir: 'I won't say that, she is just too meek, and confined to home. She has no idea about the world out there. Sherrie is well travelled. Samma, a bit closed and fixated, she sticks to her knitting. She likes to keep studying.'

Harry: 'Isn't that closer to you? To be honest, Samma, was someone I really liked, but I never made a move due to you and Freddy Uncle.'
Satbir: 'Oh my, really?'

Harry: 'She looks really sharp, and the quiet kinds.'
Satbir: 'I'm not too sure about that. Hey get to know her first. I would want the best for her. You are the best man, after me eh...?' Winking... 'but be sure you get to know her. I still don't know her. She gives up on things too fast and is occupied with the very small things in life.'

Harry: 'I have no relationship experience, and well, can be called a rookie compared to you.'

Satbir: 'When the right girl comes along, all the confidence of the world comes your way. So do not worry. Flow, go with the emotions.'

Harry: 'What was it about Sherrie?'
Satbir:'Well put simply, it's very strange, I never took notice of her when she was very young. She has come over to my place, like a million times, and we did a trillion things. As children, we played all kinds of games.' he rolls his eyes.
'I deeply remember her scared at the beach, she would stand far-away from the waves. Today, prankster that she is, she would push me into a pool, if I weren't looking. It's as if she is not the same person anymore.'

Harry: 'Then?'
Satbir: 'It became obvious I would lose her to the big wide world. And I could not face that.
She has always been around me. Yet she never made me feel that she was obsessive or clinging. She gave me the space always, and it appeared almost never took interest in me.'

Love is not...

Harry: 'What changed then?'
Satbir: 'Suddenly, I mean, besides
the fact that she turned a corner
at eighteen, and was smoking hot
during her job interview days...the
connection was something she felt.
Now this agonizing wait.'

Harry: 'Did she feel the same?
Waiting...? Airline crew, out of
sight, out of mind? Maybe she
thinks that way.'
Satbir: 'We are passed that point
now. Aren't you happy for me? I
just can't wait to see her again.
Just be with her. I treated her
poorly, collected her unread old
letters, we drifted apart. Yet, she
always kept in touch, shared her
likes and dislikes, even her
crushes on other guys. She is a
very open person. No inhibitions
and I like that about her, because
it comes across as a genuine
person.
Yet she has poise all the time, and
no pretenses with me.'

Harry: 'Lucky you, you seem to have
also played well.'
Satbir: 'No Harry, it fell in place
on it's own. It was destined. She

felt the same damn thing at the same time, and we got locked due to that.

Harry: 'Hmm..' feeling a bit dull now, with Satbir going on and on.
Satbir: 'Love is a two way thing. The reciprocity, instantaneously, when the other person can count upon you.
She cared deeply about my proximity with Samma, and that got to her, which got to me too eventually. Here was a person who cared more about us, and pointed that out - time will run out on us. We were taking each other and *time* for granted.

Harry: 'And, with Samma...?'
Satbir: 'With Samma, there was always the mystery in situations and circumstances, in choices. Not so open as a person.'

Harry: 'You seem to compare a lot'
Satbir: 'You asked??? It was like a seamless move. With Sherrie it was the mystique of her own persona, that drew me in.
Her magnetic presence, the desire she also had to be with me, and

stand by me, despite her mother. We are with each other all the time in our thoughts. It makes the wait worthwhile till her next arrival'

Harry: 'She is an attractive airline girl. You don't feel jealous? What if someone else whisks her away?'
Satbir: 'Can we keep her hiding at my home all her life? I mean she will step down for a loaf of bread and the baker will admire her. It was the same with Samma.
Sherrie has her ambitions, and we have a mutual trust. She enjoys her attention. She knows she turns heads.
I could have someone in the other room, but if she has fallen out of love with me, she could be here or elsewhere, it won't matter. I can't keep her in love with me. She must herself be in love with me. I sense that about Sherrie, and that is why, I too love her.'

Haresh: 'Absolutely?'
Satbir: 'Unequivocally. I was always very fond of her, and that was a deep starting point to crawl out of. I thought it would be slow,

but it was rather quick and sudden.'

Harry: 'Isn't she your distant relative?'
Satbir: 'Not distant anymore, eh? Look at our neighbours.
Unc.'Freddy's married to his second cousin. That's good enough for me. That man is solid.
Look at Ma. Where is my dad? Mum has always been strangely lonely and secretive all our life. I tried to rescue her from herself, but she has now gotten comfortable with her solitude. I have no reference for my love, because I never saw my dad.
It does not matter to Sherrie. She loves me. Samma asked me a hundred questions. That was the other thing that put me off. Too inquisitive, and controlling for what purpose? That too without a direction, so much information could go into a dictionary or a *How not to fall in Love* encyclopedia.'

Harry: 'You are gonna be my best man, when I have butterflies in my stomach, I'm gonna come to you for relationship advise man.'

Satbir: 'In matters of the heart, there is not much to think. Just go with the heart.'

Harry, (Voice-over) as he walks away, *'Fickle my friend, are the matters of the heart. You are blessed twice, while me, I have yet to start.'*

The light fades.

S C E N E 11 The LOVE-LETTER STAGE

The light drops on one corner of the stage.

A table is set. A pilot with very grey hair, in his uniform is seated on the side of the cafe.

Sherrie comes walking in, and takes a seat behind the Pilot. She ruffles some papers in her purse and pulls out a letter to read

Voice-over of Sherrie (Reading in her mind)

'Flashing smile,
smouldering eyes.
Burning my skin,
Heartbeat on the rise.
She never thought,
she would lose me with lies.'

Sherrie looks up, aghast, her hand over her mouth.

Sherrie (voice-over)
'What lies Satbeeeeer??'

She continues to mime the words as the voice-over continues to read the riddled-letter

'With no thought in the world,
I left her no truer,
...surely not wise.
Mercurial,
Temporal,
She swept me,
like a surge of ocean tide.
No quake,
No cracks
No imperfections,
Yet, far from fact
Only trap,
no grasp
Just a consumer of love.
With time lapse,
the gossip bit like a wasp.
She broke many
memories to mend,
a Love contract hoping to bend.

I lost you my love.
I'm told there is a man.
A Pilot with a plane to race
He at least has a chance...
So shall I give up the chase?
It will be tough,
Very Rough,
to live all over again.
After all,

Love, is not Child's Play.
Once lost,
Only a faded memory remains,
Like broken petals of a flower.
No gloss, no Shine.
they drain of colour
and power.

So it ran amok,
into the ground
like hard stone,
So, you really alone?
I'm living with rocks and pebbles,
and a heart to grind.
Neither gaiety
nor fun;
a priceless cost
I have paid
for it's you I have lost
..as I know now
it slowly slipped away.
Coz' you gave your heart away.
Love, is not Child's play.

Your ex-lover boy.

'Satbeeeeer'

P.s: Your mum has been gossiping with the
'Balsaras'- that you are having a roaring
affair with Capt. Fonseca from your
airline.

My above out pour is due to that.
Reply, to confirm the affair at the soonest
you receive this.

Sherrie: 'Capt. Fonseca!!' she shrieks.

The pilot at the back of her table reacts.

Capt: *'Morn'in* Sherrie. Here I am my dear. What is it?'
Sherrie: 'Oh sorry, Capt. I was, I mean I was reading...'
Capt: 'A love letter I reckon? Romantic fella? At which Airport is he waiting? Cmon' lets fly there on our day off. Huh?' he tries to please her with his charm offensive.

Sherrie: 'Oh Capt...! He's having doubts. Reacting to gossip. There are trouble makers on my side of the family.'
Capt: 'And why is that? Just tell them off, you only fall in love once' he sips his coffee, like any old man. Carefully, not to spill on his uniform.

Sherrie: 'My mum, she wants a wealthy groom for me.'
Capt: 'Now look here missy, if you love him, it is best you put the matter to rest, and write him a reassuring letter back. I will get

dispatch to carry it to HQ, and
from there it will go on my
account.
I have seen it all, lovers find it
tough waiting on us 'airline
people'. I still write to my wife
from every trip. So your letter
will go with mine.

Sherrie: 'Oh thank you Capt, you
are a kind soul. I am away, with a
rough roaster, for two weeks. That
will be really nice.'

She straightens out the white hotel
serviette of the Novotel Hotel Cafe in
Kuwait.

Sherrie: 'Words escape me. He's the
charmer with words.'
Capt: 'Write what comes to mind my
girl, you look like a fish out of
water. You have time till evening,
send it in a sealed envelope by 5'

Sherrie: 'Your pen Capt. Can I
borrow it?'

He hands it to her, and gets up to leave.
Sherrie begins to scribble
The light fades out...

On the other half of the stage, lights come
back on.

Satbir is seated on the sofa recliner at home.

He has a letter in his hand, that his voice-over reads for the audience:

                  Not a bird,
            that changes course.
                  not a snail,
                  that crawls.

            I am your goldfish.
      You should remember my pout,
          and that short caress,
                  -your kiss.
      As I looked at you with glazed eyes,
            from my fish-bowl.
      You always give me a shout.

                  Rescue me,
            these are cold waters.
            Or come, swim into
          the glass bowl I am in.
                  Hungry,
            in an alien land,
            Away from my shoal.

            I am *your* gold-fish
          Don't believe the sharks
          They break us, they try,
            It is easy to lie.

            Your heartbeat.
                  Cherry.

Oh Satbir, I just love you damn it. Please hold on and don't do anything terrible.

I cannot write like you in riddles. You
knew mother was never for this. Believe me,
Capt Fonseca is rich, but he is 64 years
old. A tad bit older by forty years, to get
my attention. We just serve coffee to the
senior crew. Each of us, has a loved one
back home. See you soon.
P.S.: Money can't buy me love.

Satbir, puts the letter down, reassured -
and is all smiles.

The lights fade out.

SCENE ~~12~~ ACCEPTANCE OR REJECTION?

Lights come on in Freddy's house.

Mrs. Balsara: 'Oh what a mess!'

Unc.'Freddy: Frowning. 'Why get
involved in another's affairs? I
mean that literally. The boy is
young as much as he is entitled to
choose, he is entitled to change
his mind.'

A door bell rings.

Mrs. B: Walking toward the door
looking back at Freddy, 'To be
fair, he had never made up his

mind, in the first place. Oh poor Samma.'

Mimi: 'Oh Freddy, what will I do?' she bursts into the living room, rocking Freddy's chair and sitting back on it with despondency.
Freddy: Feigns ignorance, 'Now what is the matter with you?'

Mrs. Balsara glances at him, but he shushes her up.

Mimi: 'This boy, this incorrigible boy, he seems to have fallen in love with this daughter of this terrible cousin of mine. She knows all my secrets! Now how will I face my own son?'

Mimi cries, letting out small sobs. She places both her hands on her face, hiding behind them.

Mrs. B: 'Isn't it a tad bit late to keep secrets with us Mimi?'

Freddy remains quiet, and quickly hides himself behind the newspaper.

Mrs. B: 'What is it?' Something is eating you up. You appear so distressed.'
Mimi: 'I fired Sattu, and look, he has left me a note on the dining table, that he is going away.'

Freddy: 'Away??' Freddy puts down his papers. 'My young friend is not yet a strapping young man, to just get up and leave. Where will he go?'

Mrs. B: Snatches the note from Mimi's outstretched hands and reads aloud

'Dear Ma,
As you are not in favour of my arrangement with Sherrie, and claim that the house is yours, as willed by Dad.
I have decided to step away and start my life elsewhere. Wherever I go, in the name of love, I will be able to make my life, because of the way you raised me.
Last night was too much for me to take. I know, we do not have Aunt Tiara's support either.'

Mrs. Balsara puts the letter down, and pushes her spectacles up the bridge of her nose. Mimi prods her to read on.

Mrs. B: 'Arrey what my Dikkra'

Freddy: 'Read, read'

Mrs B: (reading the letter)

*'Your complaints to Aunt Tiara,
also led her to slap Sherrie and
take her away from me.
As my father's son, I will live to
win her back, and not be able to
see you till then.
She is the love of my life ahead,
but you will always remain my
angel.
Just as one never stops loving God,
who can ever forego and forget his
mother.*

Yours Satbir.'

Freddy: 'Mimi, what did you do men?
You, you women don't think...the
young are also hot in blood, and
not short of action.'

It almost immediately, leads to louder sobs from Mimi.

Mimi: 'How was I to know, it will come to this. That Tiara has always been a gold digger. She knows the value of our house, my house.'

Freddy's face turns unpleasant but he keeps quiet.

Mimi: 'Simply looking for the richest alliance for her daughter. Shes dark and selfish, awful to steal my son away from me like this.'

Mrs. B: Inquisitively, and softly 'What is the dark secret you are so scared of?'

After moments of silence, and wiping off her tears, Mimi musters some courage to speak up, answering only to Mrs. B.

Mimi:'Oh it was a short alliance before my marriage; a relationship that did not work out. Simply because my mother did not agree to the boy. He was a devout religious student researching papers on Islamic studies at my college. Those were conservative days, but we lovers did not run away from

home like this after a petty
argument. Even though Satbir is
born out of that, that...love.'

Freddy tosses his news paper away, and
raises his hands in the air.

Freddy:'Fashions change, yet with
time, *lovers don't*. If you were
ever in love, I expected **YOU, as a
mother** to know that!! You could
have been gracious and accepted
your son's choice.'

Mrs. B: trying to soothe the blow
of Freddy's bluntness, 'It's very
common in our community in fact we
prefer a girl who is known in the
family because you know what to
expect. Look at us.'

Mimi: Snaps, and this time
addresses Freddy 'Oh, don't lecture
me about love. In our days, we
would sacrifice for the family.'

Mrs. B: 'Mimi, todays kids will not
do that. What use is your rigidness
if it turns your son away?'

Freddy: 'You can call Mrs. Tiara, and ask for her daughter's hand, what's her name... ' he trails off.
Mimi: 'Sherrie!' shoots back Mimi, cocking her head back.

Mrs. B: 'We want to eat our cake, and keep our house too, till the last day. But what use is it to you, if he is not in it? You have only one son, all of us age, and will depend on him to bring the circle of happiness back in our older lives. And why do we worry, three of us are there, we can always hole up in our house, what with us having no descendants to bank upon.'

Mimi: 'Why, where is Samma? Your foster daughter? Where will she go?'

Mrs.B: 'She has left for London for higher studies. We gave her a generous part of our savings, money that we know we cannot spend in our lifetime. Young kids do not come back from there. The ol'British hangover I must say. Your secret will remain safe with us.'

Mimi: 'I can't say that about Tiara though. She always had a mean gene and a loose tongue. Never bothers about the reputation of others, and the truth she claims, turns into a pack of lies when it comes to her own age, home and life.'

Mrs. B: Speaks as if relieved, 'My Freddy is straight as a ramrod, and *only he* is really family to me. Well that's always the dichotomy in larger family situations. They don't seem to do onto others, what they wish others do onto them.'

Mimi:'Oh all the cousins, our brothers have started their gossip. No one seems to support me; will they ever support my boy. He will become an outcast.' Mimi rubs her hands together as her palms sweat.

Freddy: continuing to cajole, 'You seem more opposed to Tiara, than her daughter actually.'

Mimi: 'Well the mother's transgressions, do more so impact the girl, won't they? Surely it does have a bearing on her nature. I must admit though, she does appear always soft before Sattu, though she looks more dusky and dark than, than,...anyways.'

Mrs. B: 'He's not really leaving the Sikh community behind. I see him regularly visit the Gurudwara, he reads his prayers, and has always been pious and so respecting to all us elders in our apartment block. He is fond of music like any young kids their age.' Mrs. Balsara sits down aside Mimi, who places her head on her shoulder.

Freddy: Conclusively...'Lucky girl. I wish my friend well. Give him *time, some space, just like we all needed it when we were young*. He is going to need all the luck in the world. I hope luck favours the brave, as he had the guts to go for it.'

Mimi: 'Yes, my child has surely grown up.'

The lights go out.

SCENE ~~13~~ TIARA'S THREATS

Lights come back on. Tiara is seated on the bed, behind Sherrie's sofa.

Sherrie: 'Ma, why don't you understand?'
Tiara: 'Why do you always have to go for low pickings. Low hanging fruit touches the ground faster.'
Sherrie: 'Ma, he has a limp.'
Tiara: 'Oh really, you noticed that? Well, he's not a cripple! As long as his equipment does not go limp...he's rich! He will inherit the petrol pumps from his father. Later years darling, its the money that counts.'

Sherrie: 'Can you let me take my own decisions for once?'

Tiara: 'You are poor in love, and could be rich in marriage. Learn from my mistakes, it is still not too late.'

Sherrie: 'We all will, won't we? And yet you and Dad will keep fighting.'

Tiara: 'I have fought your father for your flying.'

Sherrie: 'He's always been against whatever I do.'
Tiara: 'He tried setting you up with the Major from the army.'

Sherrie: 'I am not interested in service men, or petrol pump owners. I do not want your life. I do not like Dad's choices, or for that matter yours. So back off.'

Tiara: 'Don't you answer me back like this. Another tight slap will set you right.'
Sherrie: 'You cannot talk to me like this ma, I'm independent now.'

Tiara: 'It is that Sikh boy talking! Flying in an aeroplane, your feet have gone off the ground. You are nothing but a glorified waitress. How long will your young days last? It's my duty as a mother.'

Sherrie: The daughter finally confronts her (childhood past), 'Where were your responsibilities when you would leave me alone at home, and step out for your own fun.'

Tiara:'Oh shut up. Those days were safe.' The negligent mother feels a pinch of guilt, but recovers behind the facade of selfish parental control.'After all, it is for you, that I think and say what I do.'

Sherrie: Musters courage, 'You sisters have always had a different rule for yourselves, and a different one for your children. Your cousin, is harassing Sattu too because of what you said.'

Tiara: 'Oh my Sattu now! Quick to fall in love, then into bed, and faster to fall out. Huh?...' almost sneers, laughs and looks cruelly at her daughter.

Sherrie: 'You are sick, with a one track mind, I am fed-up. I'm moving out to a women's hostel on Sunday. It is better you go back to living with Dad; anyway he is your real companion, and I know you will never leave him despite all the abuse. Stop trying to control my life.'

Tiara: 'I will destroy Sattu.' threatens Tiara. The words are just out of her mouth, when her daughter nearly pounces back on her.

Sherrie: Glares back seething with rage, '*Just try it. And lose me forever.*'

Tiara: 'What is this infatuation giving you? The attraction you feel, the heat, will all disappear when you grow apart in a few years. Both of you are radically different and not meant for each other.'

Sherrie: 'Any one who loves me, makes you feel insecure Ma. You have a hard time letting go. Yet you are never there when I need you, either chasing Dad all over the country, or running behind your Richie-rich friends.'

Tiara: 'How dare you? I can really ruin it, young lady. So don't take your chances. No one knows, what I know.'

Tiara challenges her daughter, picks her suitcase, and walks out of the room.

Sherrie, worried, throws a meek surrender of a reply, '*You tried earlier and failed*. Oh Sattu, save us, from our own....'

The lights go off.

SCENE ~~14~~ DATING DAYS

The two are seated at a beach-side restaurant. He is sipping tea from a white cup and saucer, while Sherrie sits before a plate of roast chicken and asparagus, not touching her food, playing with her fork and knife.

Sherrie: 'She has not found love in her life, so she wants me to remain empty inside all my life. I have yet to see a mother like this.'

Satbir: 'Oh relax, they will both come around. Let it play out between them.' he reassures.

Sherrie: Failing to shake off her despondency, 'How can you be so comfortable? I can just faint with exhaustion thinking...'

Satbir: 'Eat something beautiful.
Otherwise imagine me carrying you
in my arms back to the hostel, all
the pretty girls there will envy
you and eye me all over again.'

Sherrie: 'They will just gobble off
the roast chicken; hungry vultures
everywhere' she throws her cutlery
aside.

Satbir: 'Enjoy my love. The feeling
of love.'
Sherrie: 'I do not feel like you.
Love is painful. It is so heavy, a
burden like a cross on my back.
Love for me is not just an emotion,
it is conflict, and all this
hatred.'

Satbir: 'You are like a feather in
my dreams, making me float
everywhere in the clouds I see, I
see you.
In the bathroom while shaving I see
you. At night in my bed I see you
in your PJ's.
Oh matrimony with Sherrie...highly
expectant this boyfriend of yours.'

Sherrie: 'How do you fit in that small room with that filthy catholic man. And then get to dream, see dreams and remember them??' she smiles at him for once.

'We started with just friends?!' she twists her nose, and catches hold of his. She offer's her hand out for a shake.

He lets out a loud sneeze.

Sherrie: 'Oh sensitive man!'
Satbir: 'The allergy to pollution, I say, its such a bummer to riding. The traffic police now want us to wear these huge astronaut sized helmets. And Michael, he's just a garage mechanic; it helps me bum off his bike, while keeping my rent down. He is a very helpful catholic man. Otherwise how do you expect me to see you so close to the airport on a working day like this.'

Sherrie: 'What happens if you lose your job?'
Satbir: 'Well I'm the highest achiever right now, so that ain't happening anytime soon for the year ahead. I'm expected to take over

from the boss, who is relocating this year to the larger head office.'

Sherrie: 'Have you met your mum?'
Satbir: 'No' he turns silent.

Sherrie: 'Don't keep the hurt within. They are our mothers after all.'
Satbir: 'You saying? They could be more understanding. I had thought, they would be the silver lining in our love, but they seem to have turned into warring foes.'

Sherrie: 'How do you know?'
Satbir: 'I speak to my friend Harry, and Unc. Freddy, they keep an eye on her. She is okay. Your mum tried to feed rumours to other neighbours but Unc.'Freddy warned them off.
Michael's Garage gives me a chance to stay solo, and blast music too, on all the stereos behind the garage. It's kind'a cool.'

Sherrie: 'So whats your plan then?'
Satbir: Pushes the plate of food before her, and hands her the cutlery. 'Have your fill of flying,

for once we get married, you gonna
have to be with me.'

Sherrie: 'I am not cooking your
meals at home, we can keep a cook
for that.'
Satbir: He looks deeply into her
eyes... 'Hey, but I need to be
cooking you right...cannot keep
waiting for three weeks all my life
to see you.'

The lights dim out.

SCENE ~~15~~ IN TRANSIT, JO'BERG,
S'AFRICA

The lights come back on.
Sherrie is seated on the sofa. Her bags
lying packed behind her. She is dressed in
her flying uniform, about to catch her
transport for her flight.
She opens a letter.

Voiceover Satbir: 'Sherrie,
It is rather alarming, that your
mum the great, has made a bid for
our house, as a pre-condition to
say yes. That means, she wants my
mother to transfer the house to
your name,'

Sherrie: 'Ridiculous!' she exclaims.

Voice Satbir: 'Interference, has its limits, but your mum takes the cake, the bus and the city too by storm. Now *obvio* – my mum has lost her cool and come and leaked all over Mrs. Balsara's sofa.
Unc.'Freddy tells me the two old women have gone bonkers and he is not referring to Mrs. Balsara who was always bonkers, but only about me. I was her Dennis the Menace.'

Sherrie: Rolls her eyes, 'Always so self-assured.'

Voice Satbir:'For my mum, I'm gonna always be centre-piece. Not furniture like, but obsession like. She gets distracted off and on, with the Balsara's foster daughter (btw- no competition here for you, shes off to London forever, go see her if you land there next time)

Sherrie: '*Meano!*' she screeches.

Voice Satbir: 'So Freddy's like our saviour, our Dad, and our well-wisher at the moment – he's all I got. Besides he's also my spy. More

next after you return from you port
of calling, or is that the back
seat of my new Yamaha?'

Sherrie: 'Can't wait
Satbeeeeeeeer!' she claims to
herself, and kisses the love letter
and places it in her jacket.

She takes her trolley bag handle and sets
off for her day's work – a new adventure
out the hotel room door.

The lights fade out.

SCENE ~~16~~ MAKE OR BREAK

Sherrie reads out of a piece of paper. In
Uniform, but minus her make-up, post a
flight date.

Satbir(voiceover):seated before her

'You had promised money,
I had promised love.
You had said to wait,
I'm tired holding onto your gait.
Are you in, or are you out?
Its time to give it a shout.'

Sherrie: She looks up. 'A poet
now?'

Satbir: 'One in the making. The
pain of your love. The separation.
My English song for you...Ms.
Hoitty Toitty.'
Sherrie: 'I had warned I was quite
a burden.' she mocks.

Satbir: 'I thought you had shed
your baby weight...'says Satbir
ruefully.
Sherrie: 'Not yet time to quit,
Satbeeeeer. Please understand.'

Satbir: 'That is our first reason
not to fight by our selves, Aren't
others enough to create that?'
Sherrie: 'Loosen up, Sattu.'

Satbir:'You have just gotten used
to your work life. Your life. Where
do I fit in? We will never be able
to buy the smallest of apartments
on Main Ave., when do we start
living together?'
Sherrie: 'Its just been three years
of flying.'

Satbir:'Three long years for me. I
have taken up an offer from

overseas, I'm flying out on
Monday.'
Sherrie:'Whattt?'

Satbir: 'London, say what?'
Sherrie: 'I can't join you. I'm
contracted to the airline and
committed to my roaster for the
next eight weeks. Its a grinding
schedule ahead, and my pay and
provident fund will remain stuck
here.'

Satbir: 'I thought we had a love
contract. I'm leaving the country
Sherrie.'
Sherrie: 'I can wait. You go
ahead.'

Satbir: 'I can't. I need you by my
side, to make a commitment, a
choice.'

Satbir is visibly hurt.

Sherrie: 'Don't do this.' Sherrie
comes and stands and leans on his
back.
Satbir:'I'm not breaking up you
fool, I want to get married.'

Sherrie: '**We** need to marry to get married Sattu.'
Satbir:'That's what I said, I need you by my side. I thought you would be happy with an overseas life. You keep flying out Sherrie.'

Sherrie:'Only to return back to home soil. This is my home Satbir.'
Satbir: 'The truth is, I don't see one, we hardly live together. I keep whiling away my time working excessively, or spending time on hobbies by myself. Where are you in my life? You do not have the *time* for me.'

Sherrie: 'Its a hard job. I believe we both will need the money to make that apartment ours. We will need to pay for a house to call home.'

Satbir: 'What's the point? See our mums – they are both left alone. It can all get done faster leaving home. Just for a while.'he pauses to take a breath of fresh air.

'Oh Sherrie, let's get married over the weekend. If you do not wish to join me in London don't. At least I will know, when I fly out, I leave my wife back home here. At her home, of her choice.'

Sherrie: 'You incorrigible soul. I'm not going with anyone else.'
Satbir: 'How would I know?'

She raises her eyebrows.

Satbir: 'Well its not exactly a level playing field for me, left standing always at the tarmac. Let them try whisking my wife away! This bloody airline of yours.'

Sherrie laughs out loud.
Satbir waits for her to settle down.

Sherrie: Responds, 'Okay! You got me.
It is a date then. Saturday. Yet, I'm not quitting my job.'

Satbir: 'Yippee, I will make the arrangements at the court. You have to just show up.'

Sherrie: 'What about our folks?'
Satbir: 'I will get the lawyer to send them an invite, like a notice.'

Sherrie:'My creative genius. Will they not dislike that?'
Satbir: 'They both have not spoken to me in person, even when I visit Freddy Unc, or you at your hostel. Your mum knows you are dating me. Stop protecting her. It should be the other way around.'

Before Satbir can crib further.

Sherrie: Responds 'I know, you feel isolated.'
Satbir: You don't?' he spits out.

Sherrie: 'I dunno, I just forgive and forget. You seem to collect.'
Satbir: 'It is the reality. I see it the way it is. The truth is, if they loved us, by now they would have got us married, rather than blocking us. They have created this huge wall of dislike between themselves. The old wall is too high for me to climb. So I will just step aside.'

Sherrie: 'Walking away, escapism?'
Satbir: 'A great escape, if you are with me.'

Sherrie: 'You always call the shots in this affair.'
Satbir: 'You set the pace in the marriage my dear.'

She puts her arms around him, over his neck. He takes her into his embrace.

The lights fade out.

SCENE ~~17~~ HOME COMING

Lights fade in for a sun-rise effect.
Lying sprawled on bed, Satbir looks at himself in the dress-board mirror.

It is early morning. A backdrop of birds in the English weather are chirping.
Sherrie is lying asleep below the sheets.

Satbir: 'For the love of my life.' he celebrates.'A letter from my friend Harry.' as he opens it up, he talks to himself.'I'm going to be a father. I had no clue, I would feel so proud. If only mother was here with us.'

'Oh why, so why did I leave my own country. My motherland. My own mother. She has yet to ever write to us. Last three years I haven't gone back home to check on her.'

A voice, his own (his conscience) speaks back to him, as if from behind the mirror.
Voice:'What choice did she leave you?'

Satbir: looks back at the mirror 'She is still my mother. I believe from Unc.'Freddy, she is in good shape.'

Voice:'Oh so you keep tabs on your mother. Love to you, is just a prison, only your prisoner changes. You can shower all your love, my pal, on that wife of yours. You were quite excited when you fell in love. At least your mother is free of you, and your irresponsible ways.'

Satbir: Talks back to the mirror- 'She must be embarrassed of me. Oh I still feel so guilty. But what can I do? I love Sherrie like the sun loves this earth, I love Ma the way the stars shine over the dark sky. Can a man not love two women at the same time?'

Voice:'She has managed to make you dance around her, wrap you around her fingers. That wife of yours.'

Satbir: 'Btw. Are you me? Or are you my mother, or Aunt Tiara actually?

Voice: 'I am your conscience. You are a bit of your mother, aren't you?

Satbir: 'In that sense, we both are.'

Voice: 'Your wife did not eventually listen to her mother.'

Satbir: 'Well, neither did I'

Voice: 'Now, that you are having a child, perhaps it is the right time to go back, to soothe the past. To bind her back into her own family. Sherrie will need her own mum. Don't you remember your own Ma, now that you will soon be Dad?

Satbir: 'I understand, this time you are right. Now can I read my friend's letter? Bugger off.'

Voice: (Harry's)...reading the letter. Satbir nods at every stage very much in agreement.

Love is not...

My friend Satbir,

Some things never change.
With each passing day, as circumstances and
priorities cast their shadows on our
relationships, our connections mature.
Luckily for me, a select few are like the blue
jeans that don't fade.

No one I know, captures the belief, that 'love
and life is energy' better than you Satbir.
Whether it was you loving Sherrie, or
befriending your Unc.'Freddy, the same passion
has been lighting up your eyes all along.

We have been friends since three decades, and
we never treated each other differently. Every
event since childhood, the Fiesta Fair, our
musical bashes, had their unique charm with you
around. You also contributed ample fodder for
the gossip mills when you were away.

You have the soul of a nomad. While home is
where the heart is, I know you are ready to
explore the world – but before that come back.
Your mum needs you, and I surely can kick you
in the butt if you are back, for chasing Samma
away.

You are the only friend, who writes to me. I
would love to have you next door again. The
Horse-Shoe Apartments await your blaring music
again.

I hope I can be the Unc.'Harry, to your kiddo.

Your Pal,
Harry.

Sherrie wakes up, and alights from her bed.

Satbir: 'Oh Sherrie, I have been wanting to ask you, will you like to go back home to have the baby?'

Sherrie: Perks up, 'Sattu, you have read my mind. I will need someone elder, either your mum, or mine. I cannot continue here any longer than we already have. London weather depresses me.'

Satbir: 'That's exactly what I was thinking today morning. But do you not want the baby to be born here, delivered and born into the system?'

Sherrie: 'Well, we are not actually giving birth to royalty. What does he or she have to look forward here, and who is going to do all the work around the baby? I will turn mad. Alone. You will go off to work.'

Satbir: 'Our mums will say we remember them only when we become parents. Let me speak to Harry, and see if I can get a transfer back home. It took effort to get this job and I cannot just give it up in a huff.'

The lights fade out.

SCENE ~~18~~ REMEMBRANCE

As the lights come on, they are all seated in Freddy's apartment.

A very pregnant Sherrie, is seated at Unc. Freddy's house.

Sherrie: 'Where is your friend Harry? Is he coming by car, or on foot from the Buckingham palace?' Freddy: 'The baby is not going to wait for time. It will come at its own time. Where is Mimi???'

Sattu walks in from the bedroom inside, sporting a moustache, the years spent in London, give him an air of sophistication, the wealth he wears on his sleeve.

Satbir: 'She will not come. Her pride is as big as Aunt Tiara's' he rallies, 'I can look for support only from Harry. My friend, my family, like you Unc.'Freddy.'

Sherrie: Wailing, 'For all the love in the world, I thought the two mothers will be on my side, when we decided to have the delivery back home.'

She rubs her hands on her belly like all pregnant women do. Inexperienced, uncertain, even anxious, but looking the part entirely. Her confidence dipping with every tug, every cramp.

Freddy: Chips in, chirping, 'If only this Mrs. Balsara had lived like a regular Parsi woman. She had to knock-off suddenly on us like this, leaving a fool like me for you kids. Of no use only I am. What man, where is this Mimi??'

Satbir: Bending on his knees, 'Freddy Unc., you have been my friend, my Dad, my pillar, and now my mother. You have given Sherrie a home. What more can I ask?'

Freddy: 'It is Mimi's loss. I do not want her to feel that I stole *her son* away. She is just across the doorway. That's the limit. The same two doors, from which you used to run up and down in our arms as a kid. We used to keep her back-up house key man!'

Satbir: 'Well, my mother is a stubborn woman.'

Freddy: Pointing at Sherrie. 'Well, lets keep her in good spirits. Tell me, what has all this meant to you?'

Satbir: 'Oh she is the love of my life. London has got us real close forever. She means everything to me. She is family, she is my friend, she is my lover, she is my end. I hope I get to go before her, like Mrs. Balsara, coz' I'm not as strong as you are.'

Freddy: '*Time* teaches you to cope, son. It is good you both got time with each other without your mums.'

Sherrie is sitting back and just listening to them.

Freddy: 'Why don't you go and help her massage her back; the doctor has seen her and informed us, it will take more time.'

Satbir gets up, and goes behind her, and gently begins to massage her.

Sherrie: 'Unc.'Freddy, do you not miss Mrs. Balsara?'

Freddy: After a deep sigh, 'Off course my dear, ours was like your kinda love. Except that she was like Satbir. She was young and so effervescent always, and I just followed her. She was the guiding light. I never decided things, she always did. It was easier that way.'

Satbir; 'Anyone before her?'
Freddy: 'Gentlemen do not speak.'

Satbir: 'Did you never fight? At least I never saw the two of you even squabble from my childhood.'
Freddy: 'We had our differences, but we never showed them publicly. Your marriage was the first time we disagreed with Mimi. Even in that we remained gentle. I think being a *Parsi* helped. We do not understand anger.'

Sherrie: 'It was still a long association?' shoulders drooping.

Freddy: 'Forty four years. When you start, you cannot see such a long pathway down the road. Initially we used to quibble about which side of the wash basin we would keep the soap, because I was left handed. But *time* carries you, and helps you to traverse over difficulties and overcome them. Eventually I learnt to use soap on my right side.'

Sherrie: 'How did you meet her?'
Freddy: 'My mother fixed it, while I was still in college. She was my second cousin, from my maternal side.'

Sherrie: 'Like us, the marriage of this kind, can become so easy, so comfortable, after the start, when you are so known to each other. How did you keep the spark?'
Freddy:'Ha, ha, it was very simple. We did not know each other that much, as we used to meet awkwardly on *Navroz* at common relatives places. We kept out of each other's hair. We spent little time in the day, but it was quality time, mostly around morning and evening tea. Her nap and meal times were

different. Till the last few years, we had all the time inside this tight apartment, but you would remember me hiding behind my newspapers from her. I would tire her her anger off, and then be ready to face her, when she had cooled down.'

Freddy longingly looks at her old photo frame. Mrs. Balsara just beams back silently from the photograph.

Sherrie, looks back-wards at Satbir.

Satbir: 'You can't hide on the internet these days. We hardly read the paper. There's the television off-course, behind which she hides, and holds onto the remote like dear life.'
Freddy: 'I tell you, this one is like me, up to some mischief?' ribs Satbir, trying to poke Sherrie out of a confession.

Satbir: Confides, 'In a way, it feels like a long time for us. Yet I feel I never left here now. And seeing you, flashes of my childhood comeback to me in this house. Mrs. Balsara always fed me so willingly.

Unc.'Freddy, having you next door was a boon since I was a kid.'

Freddy: 'I love you, *my son*. I mean, I always have loved you just like my own son. I was very careful to not steal you away from Mimi, but she would just not listen.' Freddy turns red feeling sheepish. He continues, 'You know, Mrs.B could never conceive on our own. *Ahura Mazda* has blessed you with the flame inside, the flame of your love. I'm sure the child will be born, with your spirit, and her sublime elegance and beauty. Where is this Mimi? I had informed her last night. She is one helluva rigid woman.'

Satbir looks engagingly at Unc.'Freddy, wants to say something to defend his own mother. He chooses to keep quiet as Sherrie speaks.

Sherrie: 'My pains are back. We need to leave.'
Harry: Walks in. 'Hey pal! Welcoming another Singh in the family!'

They pick up a sling-bag of clothes and walk out of the door, waiting there for a few seconds, looking back at Freddy.

Freddy: Gives them a thumbs up. 'May *Zoraster* be with you. In the fight of good and evil, love will win. See you home soon.'

The lights fade out.

SCENE ~~19~~ WAVES

Golden sun-light fades the stage back into visibility.
It's a Beach and ocean back-drop, to a mid-setting sun.

Two of them are sprawled on the beach. They are talking to each other, while a young toddler about two to three years old, is piling up sand in his pail.

In the foreground is Freddy, wearing a beach shirt, with a cowboy hat, looking silly but content and happy.

Waves lashing on the beach, (waves sound)
Harry breaks on the scene. Happy. Overjoyed look on his face.

Harry: 'See who I have brought?'

Tiara slowly comes walking in, holding
Mimi's hand.
Shocked into silence, Sattu stands up with
sand on his knees. He and Sherrie both
break into tears. Junior, is looking up at
both his parents, and then goes back to
filling sand in his pail.

Freddy: 'Oh the two old hen are
here out of their farm. Can I not
enjoy a day in the month with the
family, without drama from
someone?'

Waves lashing sound.

Mimi: 'You have been calling me
since a couple of years to return,
I wanted to wait for Tiara who was
waiting on me.'
Freddy: 'The bond of you sisters,
is stronger than even that with
your own children?'

*Satbir is still silent. He looks blankly
at Mimi.*
The look on his face is, 'Why Ma, why?'
*Everyone is looking at everyone for a
while.*
Junior continues to play.

*Mimi and Tiara walk up to their own kids,
brush their hands over their hair, and
then cross paths, as they nod at their
respective daughter-in-law and son-in-law.*

*They walk toward junior, and stop at his
feet. They crouch. Bend, and sit with him
in the sand, offering no reasons, no
excuse. The beach is too big for silence.
Waves lashing sound...*

Sherrie: Annoyed as always with
Tiara, 'How can you? Just appear
out of nowhere all of a sudden?'

*Satbir, is still looking back blankly. He
glances at Freddy, who mimes zipping his
lips. He takes it as a signal to keep
quiet himself.*

Mimi: 'Are you really able to
listen to the truth?'
Satbir: 'What do you think we are
standing here for?'
Tiara: 'I don't think they can
handle the truth.'

*Mimi looks at Freddy.
The waves, soothe down.*

Freddy: 'No Mimi, Don't!'
Satbir: Feels the air, go out of
his lungs. He bends to take the
sand from Junior's pail and lets it

slip from his hands. 'What is going on? Will you care to explain?'

He looks at Freddy, then at Mimi.

Freddy: 'Only your mother can. It is her prerogative.'

Mimi: 'It's been over thirty years Sattu. I have waited and waited for this moment, but I did not have the courage to face you earlier.'

Satbir: 'You have waited and waited? We came back from the hospital nearly three years back, to find you having left with that silly tit-for-tat note of yours. No explanation.'

Mimi: 'Well, you needed a place to stay, so our old place was ideal for you and Junior, and just like you, I have been in touch with Freddy.'

Looking at Freddy, 'You remember I had said I was going to be with Tiara, as both of us wanted you to do your own child raising. We had done our part with you two.'

Sherrie: 'Whatt???' she shrieks. 'I had no help, no guidance except for the industrious Unc.'Freddy here. And you had told him?'

Tiara: 'That was our pact. It was his turn.'

Mimi: 'To raise kids your way, you had to be away from your mums. Otherwise baby Satya here, would be his father- Satbir.'

Satbir is lost.
Freddy places his hands on his face, much the same way many years back, Mimi had.

Tiara: 'You can't handle the truth' she kicks in again.
Sherrie: Shouts out loud, 'Oh mum, just keep your mouth shut.'

Tiara: Upset, 'Really??' shrugs her shoulders, starts plying sand into the pail, and shakes hands with junior while doing it. 'Yeah, this is not my affair to explain.' She still adds, despite everyone's grumbling demeanour.

Mimi: 'It isn't Tiara.'

Moments of silence pass, The noise of the waves engulf them.
Seeing them all sit silently in the sand, Sattu thinks he gets it, but after a few seconds, he just gapes on. He looks at Tiara finally and asks

Satbir: 'Whatt???'
Mimi:'Sattu, remember me telling you about the friend I had at college, the one whom I could not see. Because of my mother.'

Satbir: Taken aback, 'Who, when? Sorry mother?'

Mimi: 'The one who wanted to study the Islamic Studies...'
Satbir: 'Oh yes, sure. But please explain why and where have you been in hiding.'

Mimi: Clarifies, 'Im coming to that.'
Satbir: 'Well..?'

Mimi: 'You see that man sitting with his beach shirt on...? He was that student from my college, whose family had faced persecution in Iran.'

It finally hits Satbir. He gets it.
And it almost simultaneously hits Sherrie.
Waves lashing sound, loudly.

'Unc.'Freddyyyyy!!!' they both
shout in unison.

Sherrie out of shock, Satbir more from a
heightened sense of exasperation mixed
with alarm.

Mimi: 'Our love was persecuted in
our own country. His Persian mother
was never keen, neither was mine.
So your favourite Aunt Balsara got
him. I was lucky he kept me as his
neighbour, so I settled for that.'

Tiara: Her commentary continues,
'That is the nature of love, if
your luck is as fickle as your
destiny. You spend years hiding,
and concealing the truth, while
raising Satbir. You were named
after that one truth, based on your
mum's-mum's customs. That was to
stay mum!'

Mimi: Continuing, 'Your grand-
mother believed in *Ek Onkar*, and
her vision of her religion, of the
clarion call...*Sat Sriya Kal*, and

all that it meant was that- 'Truth is God.' We waited for so many years, to give it to you. That was her version of the truth, of God. She did not want me to marry out of my caste and religion.'

Satbir: 'What kind of love is this? I mean, he was with Mrs. Balsara, whom I loved too, but, but...' Satbir struggles to accept his Unc.'Freddy now. 'He is suddenly Dad??' comes out of him dryly.

Mimi: 'Do you not love him as a friend already, as Unc.'Freddy. What better relationship can a father have with his son?'

Satbir: Almost sparring, 'We missed so much *time* together. We could have done so much together.'

Mimi: 'Did you not? You spent half your life in his house, rather than ours. A mother can always have more time with you too, but we went away so that you could again get time.'

Freddy: 'My friend, Mrs. Balsara never knew. We kept it that way. We were both already hurting

initially. Mimi made me understand,
that there was no reason for us to
hurt her. In that way, we were both
truly honest to our relationship.
Mrs. Balsara, was my wife. She did
not know that you existed in our
lives, before she came into mine.
And Mimi was always my first love,
and as your mum, she accepted this
arrangement. You were a permanent
symbol of a reminder of me to her.'

Mimi: Nodding, 'And that was
enough' as if to purge his father
out of Satbir's life naturally.

Satbir: 'So you decided for both of
us?'

*As it unravels, Sherrie just keeps
watching the turn of events. Then
realizes, to ask her query.*

Sherrie: 'Oh Ma, you were always
into this?'

Waves lashing softly.

Tiara: 'Sherrie, I was just trying
to shield you from Mimi's already
complex life.

Sherrie: 'But...'
Tiara: 'You would not listen. You had fallen hook line and sinker, despite all my distractions. Some were natural offers on their own, but many were set up by me.
With Freddy losing Mrs. Balsara, there was no point in hiding behind this charade and putting up these dark shades anymore.

Mimi: 'Yet Freddy wanted exclusive time with you -afraid as he was. Freddy was also depressed. When Harry told us you both were returning home, it put the wheels in motion for us to act, to think, of sharing this out in the open with you. After all, it is all one family now, and it allows *Love* to win. It's time in the sun was now.

Tiara:'Otherwise these two would be happy in opposite apartments for the sake of the Apartment Council Chief and their neighbours.'

Sherrie; 'You are my mother. Yet you hid Aunt Mimi's secret. I do not understand.'

Mimi: Takes over, almost on cue from her cousin, 'The decision for me to have Satbir, was based on the truth, not my mother's truth. It was different from my truth- that *I will never be able to fall in love again*.

Yet, there is never only one truth. Everyone's story distorts their own perspective and events do the rest. I lost my mother before you were born. There was no reason for me not to have and love Satbir, and see him grow up before all our eyes.'

She pauses, looking at Satbir intently,

Mimi: continues, 'As Tiara was the only one close to me then, I had initially consulted and shared my love story with her. Later again when I moved into the house opposite Freddy's apartment, on his suggestion, she was informed of my whereabouts. That's when we fell out of favour.'

Freddy: 'And when she wanted your apartment.' He chuckles to himself.

Tiara: 'Eventually she gave it to the two of you to live. Her sacrifice won me back.'

Mimi: 'She was jealous.'

Tiara: 'I was jealous. I was in a difficult marriage with Sherrie's father. But it all worked out. I was just mortified for Mimi. She never despised Mrs. Balsara, and all the more relied on them both as a single mum. It gave Satbir time with them both too. He naturally enjoyed that, you can see Sherrie, he's made to love now.'

Sherrie: 'I believe you!' raising her eyebrows sarcastically.

Freddy looks at Satbir and addresses him squarely.
The beach tide is low, noise slows down softly...

Freddy: 'She just bore the sacrifice alone, that of both our mothers. That of our love. We did not want to repeat that mistake when it was your time.
This time, time, or even Samma for that matter, neither would come in

the way of our love child. Mimi had already been rejected by her community. I and Marukh were still accepted by ours. We just lived in a happy space seeing you grow up. We wanted you both to also get your own bond to be strong, without my community figuring out you are my son.'

Satbir: 'What is love to one, is sacrifice to another.' remembering his jolly self with Samma. 'You seem to be controlling all our lives rather than let it progress on its own trajectory. There were no compulsions then, and I chose Sherrie myself, against all the odds you all set up.

Addressing Mimi, 'Don't you think you took it too far? The only person who did not manipulate us, was Mrs. Balsara. I suddenly miss her very much' Satbir grumbles.

Mimi: 'So do we. And we missed you'. Her arms outstretched hoping she would get a hug from her son. 'Sometimes, for the growth of your own child, you have to take yourself out of the equation.'

Sherrie looks at him, hoping he would *take this* in his stride, digest this slowly. All this while she watches over Junior who is busy by himself playing in the sand.

Sherrie: 'Undoubtedly *Mimi'Ma* has made a huge sacrifice' The weight of the conclusion dawns on all of them, except Satbir.

Satbir does not respond back with a hug. Mimi puts her arms down.

Satbir: 'I'm going back to London.' He says it so softly, it is almost to himself.

Harry: 'Satbir, slow down. You have all the time in the world. I know I once called you a nomad, but you have just got your whole family back. What are you saying?'

Satbir: Speaks softly to all of them collectively, 'What is love? You all call this love? You have kept things hidden from me all this *time*. From both of us. You call that your love for us?

Back then, you tormented us, nearly did not allow us to come together. This is your _truth_? This, this awkward relationship of next door neighbours. What a farce!'

Pointing at Freddy, 'And you, I missed you all my life. I missed my father. She kept making up the same tragic story, there were years she just lay depressed. In bed. Perhaps thinking of you, next door, hiding behind those newspapers as always. You even hid from Mrs. Balsara all the time.'

Freddy: 'Its all in the past now.'
Satbir: 'It has messed with my past, when it was the present time of day for me.'
Freddy: 'Those were simple times, and I was a meek man my friend!'
Freddy looks down. 'It is me who has let you down, not your mother'

Satbir: 'Love could have been an expression, it could have been a celebration of all of us together. And what of the _truth_ for Mrs. Balsara? She is gone forever from the face of the earth. Did you not want her to ever know? Obviously it would have broken her when she was already terminal. But did *she* not deserve the *truth*?'

Mimi: Uses Tiara's old sentence, with impatience 'She would not be able to handle the truth. You cannot go about parodying the blunt truth to someone, for whom it can be a sharp knife.'

Freddy; 'Son, love, is like this sand. It is coarse, yet soft at the same time.
So is truth. It is absolutely like what you feel right now. Like this sand, love can be dry or moist, wet, even mucky, like it is right here on this beach where you grew up. Yet, we do leave this beach here and go back to living our lives. We love it so much. We don't fill sand in our pockets and roam around.
We keep the feeling of being on the beach, within us. We kept love that way. We stayed in love. We have embraced and let go off Mrs. Balsara on that beach. Only the three people together, who have

loved each other so much will
understand.'

'As your Dad, I watched over you.
Your own love was also like this;
you came at a cross-roads, and then
time made you choose and act. If
you had not, you would be else
where with someone else. Your love,
like this sand, can be kept under
the sun and it shines. In the
moonlight it will glisten like the
silent waves at night.
Give it room to grow, to accept, to
change, and take in more
relationships as they come. For
they surely will, in other ways.
You could always have Mrs. Balsara
coming your way as your relative,
your daughter, or daughter in law
in her next life.'

Mimi: In a relaxed tone,
'Sometimes, love does not come all
at the same *time*, that you want it
to. Some win in love, some lose
their love. We salvaged what we
could. We could at least see each
other. You are *more* fortunate. Much
more.'

Sherrie: 'We are Satbir.' Sherrie, a bit afraid, as she can see a storm build up inside Satbir.

Tiara: 'Very fortunate!'

Sherrie: Continues, 'Sattu, even if they kept it under wraps, like sand under water, today, they have shared it with us and included us. If we recognize love is like sand, then right now, life is a beach.'

Satbir freezes, and he can hear his inner-voice:
When you feel the others sadness,
When there is truth,
Time stands still.
Understanding and respect,
I have felt this for them.

From them,... did I get the same?
Then there is happiness.
Then there is true love – for me.
Have they felt my sadness, have they felt my love?
Did they do enough?
Did they love me hard enough?

Sherrie: In a soft voice 'Let it go Satbir.'

Freddy: 'I have let Mrs. Balsara go Sattu. She will always be in our hearts. But the truth is, we are here, and she is not.'

Mimi: Pleads, 'Can you not accept us all?'

Tiara: 'Why do you not understand, the huge sacrifice your parents have already made? They did not even get the kind of *time together, that* you have got from each of them. The little bit of *time* you lost, Samma you let go, it got you Sherrie in your life did it not?'

Freddy comes in to the edge of the stage, holding Satbir;

The tide changes to high tide, waves lash out. (noise)

Freddy: 'It is not easy to love, to stay in love to stay committed. For your sake, your mother let you go, let you get married, let you go away so far. She never feared losing you. In fact, she actually challenged you that night to go. To marry, for she was afraid like you, for you. She knew that you would have loved Sherrie for the rest of your life, but you could have lost her.'

Satbir now turns around and stares at his mother.

Mimi walks up to him, 'Love is like that. Not always reciprocated the way you want it. Yet it chiselled you did it not? This experience, this exhilaration. You found yourselves together in London. Marriage is not easy. You needed *time* together to adjust. We stayed away for your own sake. I needed you to open your wings and soar. You would have remained a small town boy.
The time you lost with us, we lost Mrs. Balsara and overcame that. You both, overcame your crazy mothers. You have made your bond, we can see that.'

She now looks down at Tiara and Satya-junior, and bends down to hug them both.

SCENE ~~20~~ SATBIR'S MONOLOGUE

Satbir: 'I have you all at my feet.
But I feel like the same lost
child. That same lost child who was
at your feet years back. That child
on the beach, seeking love.
Just like my son. All over again.
For so many years, I have lived the
life of a loner. A lone child for
whom love was a far away dream.

Like the horizon on this beach. I
could stand here and gaze all I
want, but I could not touch that
horizon.
I reached Sherrie alone. Till
Sherrie, I was alone. I now feel
abandoned.'

'With Sherrie by my side, with
Unc.'Freddy next door. With mother
at home, with me in my own room.
There was something still missing,
I continued to feel orphaned.'

'I could never place my finger on
the pulse of love. I wrote about
it. My heart could not understand

this hidden truth you have shared today, I agree I am overwhelmed. It has blown my mind. I have lost my balance.'

'Back then, I did not know. I just waited on love. I sang and danced, recited poems, lost my self entirely in music, read Shakespeare in England. I did not find love in pieces. It hit me like a thunderstorm with Sherrie. I had found it when I was here, and after that I was just wandering about with no understanding at all. I have understood now. I have understood both life and love now.'

'How not to live like all of you, how not to be selfish like each one of you. Love, is not Child's Play, eh ma?'

Satbir is not just shaken, he is broken.

Sherrie: 'It is okay Satbeeeeeer. It is okay. Do not feel so sad.'

Satbir: He stops her extending his palm. 'It is **not** okay, it is my pain, let me consume it alone, like you in childbirth have, with me on your side. It feels that way, perhaps, for even that I do not know, your pain must be much much more. I cannot absorb it in my heart, the way you have in your body.'

Sherrie: 'Thats what makes her your mother Satbir.' she points at Mimi.

Satbir: 'I know, I hold her in no guilt, she is not in my cage, I see her free, happy and devoid of any pain. It is as if, her pain has transferred – it has come into me, her love for her child is come into me. I do Love.
I love her, like a child, like my own, it's the pain she held, she is free, it has come into me.
The love I have felt for each of you, is enshrined in my heart. Yet my heart has crumbled with these facts. I cannot join the pieces together again.
This desire to lie, almost hold the truth back, is akin to living the biggest lie of my life.
My little love did not get your attention then, to accommodate it inside your life, despite your little lie? You could carry on your

unabashed lying, while I ran to each of you to rescue me? To rescue my love?'

'It has gotten me used to walking a lone path. For the years in the immediate past, I am entrenched for survival, as much as they – yet they did not have parents, mine abandoned me for each other.
I called *Unc'Freddy* to know how my mother is? He never let me believe he was already there for her. I felt paranoid for her in London. For their own selfish purpose?

I think in the art of being alone, I'm a first class loner, kept away from your secret, your parentage, I am now truly a first class orphan. My entire life feels abandoned. It is to be born, perhaps to be a puppet to you-to take care of others, everyone else, but yourself.'

Looking at Sherrie

Satbir: 'In a few years, will we feel the same way about marriage too? Nothing lasts forever. With

Mrs. Balsara gone, this is another chapter of their lives.'

Tiara: Lets out a sob, 'Why so much of bitterness? You have my Sherrie with you!'

Satbir:'Your Sherrie, my Sherrie? Sherrie is of herself, of her son now. She belongs to him, as much as my Ma belongs to me. Sherrie has nursed, cared and raised Satya alone. Without the two of you.'

'They both were complete by themselves. Like a mother kangaroo. Till he outgrows her. Then he too will jump away like me. The *truth*, the circle of life. Oh it has all dawned upon me.'

Looking again at Sherrie

'In the end, you yourself too will out grow me. Hurriedly in a few minutes after I go, live a few seconds for yourself.
Once you become a dad, a father, did you really live for yourself *Unc.'Freddy*. Except the selfish stage of being in day to day existence.

You comforted me with your empty words, but with no embrace. You actually hugged your newspaper more. I was fooled into an existence, that you all loved me.'

Freddy: 'My friend...stop.'

Satbir: 'Your love is nothing but a blind-folded way of handing me back an empty envelope, that says at the back - 'just love yourself enough.' I have had to retreat within myself and pack things inside myself so much. It was for the day like this, **when I am not here** - like Mrs. Balsara. Others don't they miss me? They get by all they want, What a joke!

Mimi: 'You must love yourself a little. Parents do not remain forever.'

Satbir: 'Love myself? I can't, I have failed, I remained in love with you, in love with each one of you on this beach!
It has been a silly idea, but I truly have survived only on that - your hot air! All these big empty words. Criss crossing my mind, my

intellect, my thinking. Each one of you said so much it has entirely consumed me.
Done very little, yet you all, Uncles and Aunts said so much. Unfortunately, I am not made like you, and I fail to love myself. I was busy loving you all. I need someone to love me. I needed someone then, and I need someone now.'

Tiara: Asking Sherrie,'What has come over him? Has he not recovered from post-natal depression rather than you?' Her joke falls flat, and no one smiles an inch.

Sherrie; 'Ma, there you go again with your hand and foot in mouth disease. Can you speak lesser than normal?'

Tiara: *Breaks down into inconsolable sobs*. 'My life has been a waste, a failure with every relationship.'

Mimi: Crying out loud, embraces Satya (Satbir's son.)

Freddy consoles her.
The sound of Waves lashing...

Satbir: Vomits out 'Since you two have each other now, why do you need us?'

Sherrie: Exclaims, '*Satbeeeeer*. Can you show some grace?'

Satbir: 'I cannot. It is the naked truth, isn't it. Lying bare on the beach here. Sunbathing before the clouds and the waves. I cannot believe *this* is where I spent my childhood with them?. I will not let him spend his here.'

Waves lashing sound...
He bends forward, with Tiara trying to hold him, he heaves past her, lifts Junior up in one swing motion. He cradles the child in his arm.

Satbir: Addressing Satya his son,'I will love you my son, as no one has loved any before. You are my friend. My love, my son. The needle of love, has shifted. Away from all these people.'

Love is not...

As he walks away in a huff, Sherrie chases behind him. They both go off stage, with Satya.

Sherrie: 'What have I done? Why are you upset with me?'

Left sitting on the beach are Tiara, Freddy and Mimi.
Freddy pats Mimi on her head affectionately, and settles her hair, as they fly in the light wind.

Freddy:'You can make one mistake as a parent, and all the good is down the drain.'

Mimi: 'The nature of love, disappointed?' she asks.

Freddy: 'The nature of truth.' he responds. 'I warned you.'

Tiara: 'The passage of time. It heals all wounds'

She gets up, and sits on the lounge chair at the beach, facing the sun. She takes the centre one. The other two join alongside. Waves lashing sound...

Freddy: 'Two's company, three...'

Tiara: 'Not the best triangle, we would make.'

Freddy: 'We won't let you either. I have just found my love back, as has my son.'

Mimi; 'I have just lost mine. I had told you the truth Tiara, even so many years back, with much hesitation. That *truth* stands tall till date, and will stand the test of *time*.' She lets out a sigh, I knew it... '**Love** is Not Child's play. *Someday*, Satbir too shall come to know of it.'

Tiara: 'Since a young age, you have been indifferent.'

Mimi: 'Everyone does not interfere like you with their kids.'

Freddy: 'From a young age he always wanted the truth, however bitter or ugly. Give him time, he will eventually digest the truth.'

Tiara: 'Oh they will be back, if they love us folks. You know that,

I know that. They always come back.'

The lights fade out,...
(Audience expecting an end?)
Chopin Raindrops/...Piano music

The curtain drops.
Gradually lights come on...two corners of the stage.

SCENE ~~21~~ CLOSING ACT: VISITING DAD

Satbir (*With his pencil thin **greying moustache***) and an **aged** Unc.'Freddy are standing on two ends of the stage.

Satbir: Whipping out his cellphone. 'Unc.'Freddy, can I call you that still? Dad does not seem to stick in my head.'

Unc.'Freddy: 'Sure champ. No difference to me. When do you arrive from London?'

Satbir: 'Do not come to the airport, I will see you at home.'

Freddy: 'Sure my friend. Is Sherrie flying in too?'

Satbir: 'No Dad. She's in Amsterdam now, gone back to the Airlines. We are no longer together. Training to become a co-pilot. Her mother was right about us. How you coping without mum now?'

Freddy: 'It's been three years now she is with you after all. Left me for you. You are her angel, she cannot live without you.'

Satbir: 'She is happy to be back with her son. True that. Okay then, more when I meet Unc.'Freddy, C ya...after this weekend.'

Satbir bites his lower lip, and disconnects the call.

Satbir: 'He must really miss mom and Mrs. B...' he trails off. He calls aloud 'Samma, I will be back in London in a week.' His phone falls.

Samma: Stepping out on stage, 'Still dropping things, all these

years,...apples, now phones. Apple
i-phones.'

She picks up his phone and the suitcase.

He shrugs, gives her a peck on the cheek,
and lifts the curtain, to step back inside.
Samma follows.

A voice-over: *'Freddyyyy...'*

Freddy: 'Yes my luv?'

Voice: (noise...walking steps from
behind the curtain) 'Are we going
to the beach after all?' pops out
Tiara.

Freddy: 'Yes, my luv. After all,
truth and time wait for no one my
luv.'

Tiara: 'Is there anything called
love, my luv?'

Freddy: 'Like Father, like son',...
'that my luv, is Love.'

Curtains it is.

End of Play.

INTERVIEW

08-August 2023.

Love is not...

In this play, 'Love is Not Child's Play' you dear reader, would have noticed, there are two lovers, two neighbours, two friends and two cousins, beside two female love interests that embody fondness v/s infatuation.

These 'couples' set the ball rolling in two's for a compact cast to deliver the story from the eyes of *Satbir's <u>truth</u>*.

There is no city location context, except a beach. Sattu could be the boy next door, caged by his solitude in any apartment around the world.

The <u>time</u>, is somewhere in the 21st century when aeroplanes changed the way we saw the world and worked.

What led sun:jeev to write this play, let's zone into understanding the man, behind the author.

An interview with sun:jeev follows.

Q: Why a play, for your third sojourn?
A: I have been meaning to write one since long, in our young days, I used to visit Prithvi and Bhaidas hall (BOMBAY) to view live performances. In college, I was always back-stage. My wife also loves Shashi Kapoor, who was the force behind Prithvi.

Q: So when did this play find it's origin?
A: Honestly, in Bombay of the 90's and some memories of watching other plays.

Q: Do you get asked this often, why the colon in your name?
A: My mother made me realize the power of my name. To 'stay always alive.'

Q: Any inspiration?
A: Life itself. Love. Family and friends. The experience of others. twist of fate...so many things. Published works and anything creative, the ocean, mother nature, the beach.

Q: Why do your characters often meet, separate and reunite? At farms, hills, at the movies, in trains and planes. Even stations and airports.
A: I try to retain a slice of life. We all come and go. I try to capture the impact of people's movement, travel. Even migration or homecoming. It creates stories. Otherwise people can be boring, and I rather write about interesting characters lives.

175   **Love is not...**

Think about it, some people stay indoors,
but many others, are rarely found at home.
Humans make a hullabaloo to make a home,
but they work and spend their time outside
it.
An actor, a farmer, a labourer, a priest, a
teacher, a child. Will you find them at
home easily?

Q: What was the challenge to write a story
for stage?
A: When you write, as a playwright, you do
not have the liberty of the back-story, or
a character's background. You can play with
the background score, music, sets, even the
costumes or props.
The stage audience has lesser preparation
than the reader of a conventional fictional
novel.
The director can tone down or amp-up the
drama. It can be more fun, or tragic,
leaves a lot to interpretation – of the
enacting actors and audience.

Q: Any unique elements or context in this
story, compared to your earlier books?
A: The passing fancies with time, the
coming of age of a young boy, into adult
hood and then family.
Yet no context of time period or specific
location where he lived, besides an
apartment. The beach is his child-hood
home.

Q: What is the premise you kept, to create
Satbir's character?

A: The main thing is that he has grown up without a father, and is seeking something, he discovers 'Love by accident, all of a sudden.'
It was my working title. He is a feelings-metrosexual guy.
He can go for anything, and is the sorts, to go in any direction, is open. He responds to emotion. What he does take time to realize is that others could also go for anything.

Q: From where do you get the women in your stories?
A: Writers watch women, men, everyone. There is also one's imagination. As long as there is consistency in the graph of story-telling, a message, or sometimes, the turn of events, dreams, music. I am also a bigger reader, than a writer. Its the best way to self-motivate.

Q: Many writers from India, write stories that are either Indian, or those of overseas Indians.
A: My first novel is a very Indian story. Yet, it can educate foreigners about India over a seventy year period. My oldest reader was 91 and the youngest 17. The second novel was more a today's pace the fake international life of NRI's and how you can repair yourself, survive or perish. This one aims to be sheer drama, as dramatic as anyone's hidden truth.

Q: Anything more we can expect.
A: Poems, they have been long in cold storage and the inner recesses of my mind.

I hope to work on collaborative short-stories with other new writers. I'm on instagram and FB, email etc. Give me a shout.

Q: What do you think about publishing with bigger brands?
A: A new author struggles too much. I just concentrate on writing. That is my focus as of now. There is solitude and immense freedom, so it is very enjoyable. To create in the same way you read, it is your pick and you are alone. I'm waiting to be discovered.

Q: What gives you immense satisfaction?
A: The completion of a story. After I have put it down, the editing takes weeks or months, that does not bother me.
It is when a story is brewing to come out, the nervous energy around writing – mostly through late nights. It is very liberating and exhilarating, when you finish, the first draft. Next morning you are bleary eyed, and still keen to improve immediately. The first draft to the next various versions, just consumes you. Even if a few thousands read your book, you are your own first reader, and it feels great that you have created something for other potential readers.

Q: How much time does a book take?
A: The working on the draft can be a nine to ten month process for me, the fastest has been twenty five days for me to write – the second novel. It was living inside my head for years, but I was searching for

context to put the story in. The conceptualization takes years, and collection of material and observations are very important to any writer. Characters names, and research is also important. Many feel the title and cover-page is the most difficult task, I usually seal that in a day. Every writer does things differently. Usually a book every year is a good rate of progress.

Q: What do you see in the future for yourself?
A: Infinite opportunities.
I have lived that way.
I could change track. Maybe even keep just writing for another two decades. I do not know. I'm hoping it leads to a script or a film story someday.
As you write more, you get better. My attempt is to create different kinds of books each unique from the other.
I encourage all prolific readers to write, but they prefer hiding behind a book, or a TV, rather than a pen or a computer. It is what you enjoy and what you seek, as well as what you put in front of yourself, that can inspire to create.

Q: Whose work impresses?
A: Oh that's a long list.

Q: Share a few titles/authors who impressed you, and led you to writing
A: I first published a novel in 2020. It was due to covid, that was the impetus. It felt, life may come to an end, and I want to leave something behind for others. I wanted to do it in the space of fiction,

and yet did not want to distort reality entirely to make it insensitive or senseless. So I gave myself a very limited brief, and kept Guru's of Literature (My book collection) in mind,

I believe, those wanting to explore the Indian character storylines would most enjoy Indian origin authors like Amitav Ghosh, Rabindranath Tagore, Devika Chitra Banerjee, Arundhati Roy, Jhumpa Lahiri, and Vivekananda.
I am also deeply impressed by Toni Morisson, Anita Desai, Murakami and Han Kang, though I have not read all their works.

My father used to say, 'Twenty four hours are too less for a reader', I think- 'imagine being a writer of the calibre of the above inside those hours.' I just wish to leave something behind for my kids, it started that way, and I think I have gone beyond that now, to push my own self to tell interesting stories.

By choice, I mostly read awarded authors. Otherwise out of curiosity I pick books only based on titles and their covers.

Then there is an entire space over a century before us, which is not easy to find and grasp, and there's always the English poets and playwrights; it's a schooling of sorts- Oscar Wilde, Rudyard Kipling's short stories, Hisham Matar's In the country of men, Anton Chekhov works.

Love is not...

I also forgot to mention- everything
written in India by Perumal Murugan,
Khushwant Singh, Kiran Nagarkar and
Gurcharan Das.

Q: How do you create? What is your way of
preparation?
A: I do not know. It is on going. It never
ends, it's like moving toward infinity.
Thoughts just come to me, It may sound
strange, I do not think when I write – it
is coming from the subconscious mind, like
dreams.
Maybe it is by creating creative
discipline. Input-output. I do not waste
time watching televised trash. It was pure
joy reading simple comics alone as a kid, I
still enjoy that at times, it refreshes
you.
The illustrations of Tintin blow my mind.
The days of Hardy Boys, Enid Blyton and my
childhood Commando Comics is over. Yet, it
feels like yesterday. I still have a
graphic comic, or desire to read Enid
Blyton's Famous Five over and over again.

Q: Future ambition?
A: No, to be able to write more, and get
huge city space in the centre of the city,
to open a Library. It will be a dream come
true.
Libraries are a social need, as they equip
the current generation for the future – at
any time, and helps them get a reference to
connect with the past. 'The Gospel of
Wealth' by steel magnate Andrew Carnegie,
made America great. He inspires.

Q: Your top three literary choices?

A: Perfume by Patrick Suskind, I discovered it on a trip to Vancouver, for $2. It made me feel wealthier than many years of overseas life and riches. That is the power of reading.

Kiran Nagarkar's Cuckold, a terrific Indian gem, that gave me many a conversation with my father about becoming a writer, and owning a Library some day. We used to discuss awarded books, and scourge newspapers to unravel new and old titles. The third would be 'The Difficulty of being good' by Gurcharan Das, that left an imprint on my heart and soul. It is the modern day interpretation of the B'Gita.

Lastly, I would love to add a gem, a translated work, 'Rainbow at Noon' on the story of failed renunciation, by Dhiruben Patel.

Love is not...

Love
is
N O T
Child's
P L A Y

"Life is a beach. Love is like sand, soft and coarse at the same time. But then, so is truth. Like love, truth and time, wait for none."

Satbir is the proverbial happy child, to a lone mother Mimi. Under the loving umbrella of his neighbours -Mr. and Mrs. Balsara, 'Sattu'. grows up being a loner, with a solitary friend Harry. It is Unc.'Freddy next door, who plays the loyal neighbourhood chum, in the absence of Dad.

The generation before Satbir, has performed many a sacrifice and penance to deliver themselves from love. Mimi is mother to the devoted son, keeping something secret to share many years later. Their small family of two, is hit with change, when Aunt Tiara and her *daughter* come back into his life. Will **Samaya** stand a chance? Or will *Sherrie* sweep him off his feet?

It is now for Satbir to choose the girl of his dreams, to get it right, and keep his family out of the triangle. It gets muddy and sticky, like the wet sand on his childhood beach. It takes a lot to understand what love is, after all LOVE is NOT Child's P L A Y.

Love is Not Child's Play-is written as a timeless story, for theatre. The swings in *fate and cupid* give ample opportunity to stage the drama. Sure, there's always a musical reference by sun:jeev to set the mood.

About the Author

sun:jeev is the nomDePlume of Sanjeev Bhatia, who resides currently in Bombay, India.

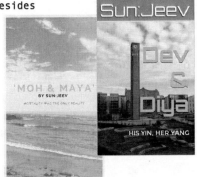

This is the author's first play, and his third work of fiction, (the first being Moh&Maya and the second, Dev&Diya.) **The play explores the** tangibility of truth and time, **and their impact on love.** The way Satbir receives, feels and interprets love, is different at different times, converging to his truth.

The earlier work of the author (Moh&Maya) explores a Mother's affection, the Maya of attachment and the illusory love (moh) for her land, her house, her sons, - the impact of family migration and a pandemic on her choice. The second book (Dev&Diya) looks at the lost cause of George's fatherhood, covered with themes like jealousy and infidelity affecting the physical, human and mental condition.

Love is not...

Manufactured by Amazon.ca
Acheson, AB